A Writer's Statements on Beauty

A Writer's Statements on Beauty

New & Selected Essays & Reviews

Wally Swist

SHANTI ARTS PUBLISHING
BRUNSWICK, MAINE

Published by Shanti Arts Publishing
Interior and cover design by Shanti Arts Designs

Shanti Arts LLC
193 Hillside Road
Brunswick, Maine 04011

shantiarts.com

Cover and interior images: istockphoto.
com/165765272-3; istockphoto.com/165765917

Printed in the United States of America

ISBN: 978-956056-36-5 (softcover)

Library of Congress Control Number: 2022935226

For the Readers of These Essays & Reviews
& for Tevis Kimball

Contents

Acknowledgments

These essays and reviews previously appeared in the following anthologies, compendiums, online magazines, and print journals, often in earlier versions.

Adelaide Literary Magazine: "Novel as Painting: *The Tiger's Wife* by Tea Obreht" and "Revisiting *The House of the Spirits:* Mysticism, Love, and Magical Surrealism"

Connecticut River Review: "Michael Miller's *Darkening the Grass: The Transcendence of Death*"

Grolier's Masterplots: "The Novel as Fictional Autobiography: *Loitering with Intent* by Muriel Spark"; "*If on a winter's night a traveler:* Italo Calvino's Contemporary Allegory and Literary Pyrotechnics"; "Compression, Sparseness, and Lucicity: Raymond Carver's *What We Talk about When We Talk about Love*"; "The Modern Tragedy of Marriage: *Life before Man* by Margaret Atwood"; "Comprehensive Biographical Scholarship—Uncovering a Secret Life Well-kept: *Maughm* by Ted Morgan"; "Enigmas and Scapegoats, A Superior Work of the Imagination Grounded in Actuality: *Black Tickets* by Jayne Anne Phillips"; "Integrity, Craft, and a Touch of the Marvelous: *The Poems of Stanley Kunitz, 1929-1978*'; and 'A Prehensile Language and the Geographical Terrain of Body and the Mind, *Selected Poems* by Margaret Atwood"

The RavensPerch: Adding Breadth to Words: "Anonymous Gifts" and "Der Blaue Reiter Group, Steven Schroeder, David Breeden, and Daodejing"

Today's American Catholic: "On Gratitude: Persevering through the Coronavirus Pandemic"; "On Guidance"; "On Inner Prayer: Constantly Changing Gifts"; "On Presence: The Commonplace We Can No Longer Remember" and "On Presence and Love: The Opening of the Heart"

Your Impossible Voice: "Just to be a Silken Thread Woven into a Grand Design: *Etudes: A Rilke Recital, Translations and Commentary* by Art Beck"; "Translating Ungaretti"; "As Much Beyond Music as Harmony Transcends Speech"; "To Be Both Body and Spirit: *The Angled Road: Collected Poems, 1970-2020*"; "Review of *The Art of Prophecy: A How-To Guide from Beyond the Grave by Amos, a Major Minor Prophet* by

David Breeden"; "The Chapbook as High Art: *The Insistent Island*"; "Art Beck's Translation of M. Valerius Martialis' *Mea Roma: The Poetic Practice of Erudition, Sophistication, and Urbanity: Martial: Mea Roma: A Meditative Sampling from M. Valerius Martialis* by Art Beck"; and "Intellect, Essences, and End Rhyme: James B. Nicola's *Wind in the Cave* and *Natural Tendencie*s"

"D. H. Lawrence's *Women in Love*: Seeking What Is Beyond the Realm of What Is Human and What Is Humanly Divine" and "Revisiting *The House of the Spirits*: Mysticism, Love, and Magical Surrealism" were commissioned articles initially published with EBSCO, an academic library research database, in an entirely different format, but appear here in a more polished, updated, and revised form.

"D. H. Lawrence's *Women in Love*: Seeking What Is Beyond the Realm of What Is Human and What Is Humanly Divine" was collected in the *Adelaide Literary Awards Anthology: Essays 2019* (New York & Lisbon: Adelaide Books, 2020).

"Translating Ungaretti" was collected in the *Adelaide Literary Awards Anthology: Essays 2020* (New York & Lisbon: Adelaide Books, 2021).

Author's Note

This collection of essays and reviews has been compiled to extend and complement the work collected in *Singing for Nothing: Selected Nonfiction as Literary Memoir* (Brooklyn, New York: The Operating System) and especially as a companion volume to *On Beauty: Essays, Reviews, Fiction, and Plays* (New York & Lisbon: Adelaide Books).

The essays and reviews offered herein in Parts One and Two were written recently—within this decade (2010–2021) or so, and often enough just within the last three years (2019–2021). The reviews appearing in Part Three are selected from work written in previous decades. Since this earlier work did not signify itself as being dated and rendered itself still pertinent, the author found that work, after much deliberation, significant enough to collect in this volume to segue and contribute to the overall themes and ethos of this book—as a literary work of aesthetic and social consequence.

Wally Swist
South Hadley, Massachusetts

PART I

Gratitude, Guidance,
Presence, and
Inner Prayer

On Gratitude

Persevering through
the Coronavirus Pandemic

IF WE PRACTICE LISTENING TO OUR INNER voice and are disciplined in this practice, we can open ourselves to be able to listen to guidance. When listening to guidance, we enter an inner quietude that is accompanied by a distinct sense of astonishment for being present in the moment, which is how we began listening to our inner voice, which then led to listening to guidance. When we are present, there is yet a fuller depth that we enter, and that depth allows us to become awash in active gratitude.

Active gratitude is the awareness of our interconnectedness with all things and with each other. However, in experiencing this awareness we also become more aware of our gratitude for everything and anything that we are touched by or that we touch. And the list can be consequential. Walt Whitman and his endless lists within poems such as "Song of Myself" in his visionary and ageless *Leaves of Grass* come to mind—certainly to the scrutiny of his critics. Those same literary critics missed the inherent spirituality to be found there. Despite their critiques, contemporaries of Whitman, such as Richard Maurice Bucke, knew Whitman personally and also wrote a monograph on him. Bucke, who is known for his groundbreaking book, *Cosmic Consciousness: A Study of the Evolution of the Human Mind*, offers substantial claims in his monograph that Whitman had, beyond a doubt, broken through into an awakened state of being.

We can begin simply by listing our gratitude during the Coronavirus epidemic by what we miss: our weekly excursion to the local library; our interaction with our favorite grocery clerks who may have been moved to other shifts, are pulling double shifts, or are working different days; our not being able to walk the paths on our local college campus due to shutdown; or our not being able to walk through public parks or on the trails of nearby nature areas. Being shut in means we need to listen to ourselves, and as Hercule Poirot might say, "to the little ticking of the clock" (from Agatha Christie's *The Clocks*). However, if we can begin to practice active gratitude, we can start to access something altogether different, something that perennially enriches us, and something that can become active within us; this something is awe and astonishment for each moment of every day, and this practice can be described as finding the numinous in the everyday. Becoming aware of the ever-changing present moment in such a way offers nothing less than active gratitude, if not even a kind of magnetic sense of direction, a north star, a true north—and, yes, we can even call such direction a moral compass.

This brings to mind a character who may be the most significant in all of English literature regarding moral compass, and that personage is Gabriel Oak from Thomas Hardy's monumental novel, *Far from the Madding Crowd*. There are some nineteenth-century writers who remain modern, and these include Henry David Thoreau, Emily Dickinson, Walt Whitman, and most certainly, Thomas Hardy. If *Far from the Madding Crowd* isn't a novel that regards the awareness of gratitude and the active practice of it, then I'm uncertain what other novel offers such a fine example.

Gabriel Oak is one of the most formidable characters who embody a moral compass. Hardy introduces us to him as a sheep farmer, one who is thriving, the owner of a large flock, in full competence of himself and of the knowledge of the land on a ledge above the ocean on which he lives and loves. When he sees the ravishing Bathsheba Everdene, who is working on a local farm with a relative, the spark of eros is struck within him, and he proposes to her. In keeping with her fierce independence, she refuses him; however, this is not the end of their relationship with each other but just the beginning.

As we might be blighted in whatever myriad of ways during the Coronavirus pandemic, Gabriel Oak loses all of his sheep one night when one of his sheep dogs (he has two named George, and this one was the crazy one) drives all of his sheep out of their pens then herds them off the sea cliffs into the breakers below. Despairing but not quite distraught, Gabriel Oak moves on to a large farm, which by now Bathsheba Everdene has inherited, and just in passing saves the large barn from burning down due to an accidental fire beginning in one of the hay lofts. Bathsheba offers Gabriel a job, and the story continues on from there, with Gabriel practicing not only care and love for Bathsheba through his saving an entire harvest on her wedding day from an oncoming storm by tying tarps over the stacks of grain to persevering with her through a doomed romance that he had predicted would be wrong for her.

Gabriel Oak is sturdy in his moral compass. He never deviates from his course, not even once, but perpetuates in his practice of active gratitude — he may not have had Bathsheba's hand in marriage, nor her promise of that happening someday, or even entertaining, as he had to weather, her not ever becoming his betrothed — still he stood firm in his conviction to love and care for her, to make sure the farm was succeeding enough that he might even think of leaving it after the doomed marriage with the cavalry officer was finally finished. But it is, of course, then that Bathsheba eventually comes to the conclusion that Gabriel is someone whom she does love and a man strong enough not necessarily to tame her but to ride alongside and to endure to be her equal — as well as he being hers. Gabriel Oak is a necessary hero in our age of a sheer lack of heroes; however, moreover, he is a practitioner of active gratitude since he did lament what he didn't have but opened himself to the level of the heart and became aware of his interconnectedness with all things and to all people, which is, if anything, a Whitmanesque notion and vision.

The eminent psychologist and psychiatrist Carl Jung, who is the founder of analytical psychology, stated at the end of his long life that he thought he had made it as far as the fourth chakra, which is the heart chakra. Of course, this is the level of the heart, and this is also the practice of active compassion. Joseph Campbell, noted expert of comparative religion, calls this activating of the fourth chakra moving "out into the marketplace as Christ did' on a daily basis, and if this is not also practicing active gratitude for our interconnectedness with all things and all people, especially during these trying and challenging days of the Coronavirus epidemic, at least figuratively, and even within the confines of our own homes, but with an open heart, then we will have missed a golden opportunity to progress during these changing times, to coalesce during a time we have to become that much more evolved not only as human beings but to veritably advance our souls toward a growth of awareness and consciousness that is, above all, our birthright.

For each of us who moves forward in this way, there must surely be a light that blinks on for each consciousness that is raised for everyone across the globe, as Manjushri, a bodhisattva in Tibetan Buddhism, and the channel who informs Penny Gill an Emeritus Mount Holyoke College professor, in her book *What in the World Is Going On?:*

Wisdom Teachings for Our Time. And to just imagine not only just our own practice of active gratitude informing such an event but that our collective active gratitude could possibly change the world is more than enough for us to consider beginning our practice, unhesitatingly, not just sometime today but at this particular moment — *this one* that is so rich in such a nascent and distinctly wondrous world of possibilities.

On Guidance

THE THOMAS GOSPEL OFFERS US GUIDANCE in what is an essential understanding of our lives, when it states toward the end of the text that "the Kingdom of Heaven is spread across the earth but men do not see it." This, like all guidance, is not only worth noting on a daily basis but these words can offer us a daily meditation and daily practice. Seeing the world differently, with more of an intrinsic radiance, is practice, indeed, during dark times and periods of providence. However, as the German poet, Rainer Maria Rilke, suggested it is in first living the questions do we ever arrive at integral answers to our questions; and the questions clearly form before us as to how do we return to seeing that "the Kingdom of Heaven is spread across the earth" and that women and men "do not see it?" as well as what exactly is guidance and how do we go about listening to it?

Thirty years ago, I began a mindfulness practice of listening to my inner voice. For some twenty years before this I had observed that my inner voice was never faulty, never wrong, and always pointed to a veritable true north whether regarding moral, practical, or spiritual questioning. For some twenty years, my practice was to develop my vigilant listening to my inner voice. This was daily practice, which mirrored silent prayer practice. Silent prayer practice can be instituted while driving to work, standing in line at the grocery store, or while washing the dishes. Silent prayer practice can also be mindfulness practice. Mindfulness practice can be "taking care of the horses," as the British spiritual philosopher Russel Williams did for some three years before he experienced a rather extensive spiritual awakening but it can also be a daily practice, especially if it leads to such an awakening. However, the basis of such spiritual discipline is in vigilant listening—and that begins with listening to your inner voice.

About ten years ago, I began to move on quite intuitively from listening to my inner voice to the practice of presence. The practice of presence evolves from listening to your inner voice but it is a broader, deeper, and richer experience. Presence itself can also include a daily prayer practice (such as The Jesus Prayer, modified such as "Lord Jesus Christ, have mercy on me" or you can pray for another as in "Lord Jesus Christ, have mercy on my wife, etc.") or it can be as simple as Russel Williams "taking care of the horses," but the essence of presence is in living in the moment. This may sound easy to do, and it may eventually become a practice we can keep going and facilitate most of the time, but it is a practice, and by definition practice is arduous—by nature.

Concomitant to my moving into presence about a decade ago, I also began to experience what I have come to describe as listening to guidance. Listening to guidance differs from the resonance of your inner voice in that because you are practicing presence more often than not you also become attuned to listening to guidance, most specifically because this resonance distinctly is heard from outside of your mind and body—in fact, you hear it coming from outside of your mind and body since you have become present enough to listen to such guidance. Such guidance is sometimes heard but also such guidance moves you into sublime action—as if by invisible hands.

The last decade, and more, has been my "Blue Period." As in the case of Pablo Picasso's phrase, "Blue Period," these years have been pervasive with an expansive creativity in which I have composed and finished nearly two dozen books of substance and substantive size: both prose and poetry, in various genres. I can't certainly claim that I have been the recipient of automatic writing, as at least on occasion William Butler Yeats did; and I also can't posit that my aesthetic practice has been channeled, with myself having channeled the work itself. But I do actively discern that I have been listening to guidance in much the same way I have practiced the mindfulness of hearing my inner voice, and being present enough in daily life to really listen to what thoughts and feelings my partner is expressing to me, for instance, which all leads to an accrual of grace in my hearing guidance, whether it be what it is that I write, or what decisions I make during each day, that lead not just to my own health and benefit but more significantly the health and benefit of all those I come into contact during the course of the day.

That daily practice opens you to listening to guidance and that listening to guidance showers you in active grace is not just a perennial philosophy but an active spiritual boon. It's all about the practice, though. "It's all about the work," [Pierre-Auguste] Renoir claims in the eponymous 2012 film by Gilles Bourdos, since it was Renoir's practice ever since he was a painter of porcelain china plates, indeed, to honor the ardor of work. Since it is in the ardor of work itself can we discover the seam in our lives in which we can be present enough to listen to guidance, and experience what St. Thomas illustrated in his epigrammatic phrase of "The Kingdom of Heaven" as being "spread out across the earth" in such an ostensible radiance that "men do not see it." What St. Thomas is saying is: "See the radiance." And we can, indeed, see it each day and every day. That is if we cultivate our practice of listening to guidance, since our eyes then also open to the grace that abounds within and without us.

It is not only our responsibility to learn the practice of vigilant listening for our own benefit but also, most specifically, to learn and institute this practice for the sake of all those around us—our loved ones; our families and friends, including those individuals with whom we may not always be in agreement; and everyone else who enters our lives—so we may experience our eternity here and now, most especially, and, as I try to describe in one of my own poems, "The Map of Eternity," that just is:

> [that] moment of the ineffable, one in which
> I would come to be aware that
>
> the map of eternity was only beginning
> to spread out in all directions.

On Presence

"The Commonplace We Can No Longer Remember"

"THIS IS THE BEGINNING," I THOUGHT WHILE taking the left turn off of Bay Road onto South East Street in Amherst toward the farmhouse in which I have my writing studio. I thought that in respect to the last fifteen years and the girth and depth of work I have produced there. I also thought about the passage of that time and the time after—my time after that moment while driving and this moment in which I write.

Jack Gilbert, whom I knew as a friend, and would visit at Fort Juniper, the Robert Francis homestead, where I would also be a writer-in-residence several years later, wrote in a poem, "Highlights and Interstices," some of my favorite lines, especially in regard to presence: "We think of lifetimes as mostly the exceptional/ and sorrows. Marriage we remember as the children,/ vacations, and emergencies. The uncommon parts./ But the best is often when nothing is happening./ The way a mother picks up the child almost without/ noticing and carries her across Waller Street/ while talking with the other woman."

What Jack writes further along in the poem truly does ignite the rigorous philosophical question of "What if" we "could keep all of that?" I often think of those two women on the corner of Waller Street in San Francisco and of that moment, an inadvertent moment, one in which we very well may be fluidly at one with our life and the lives of others, and without consciously realizing that we are blissfully in harmony and fully in accord with the world.

It is in that particular mother picking up her child "while talking with the other woman" who is part of the event of harmonic consciousness itself in which we discover, whether we are even partially aware of it or not, our presence in the moment. For Jack, it was an *aha* moment, often referred to as the haiku moment by practitioners in the English language haiku genre, of which he knew something about since he was married to a Japanese woman, Michiko, whom he actually names later in this poem. It is that moment I refer to as finding the numinous in the commonplace.

Later, in "Highlights and Interstices," Jack writes that he has "lost" several "thousand habitual breakfasts with Michiko." And then he furthers the idea in his conclusion a premise I don't agree with and would like to use here, in refutation, as my own premise, by his concluding that: "What I miss most about" his wife "is that commonplace I can no longer remember." Why I refute this is that Jack, as all we often do, is missing what he so brilliantly wrote in the first half of the poem—and that regarded the active presence of those two women on Waller Street, who are completely at one in the moment, and in their doing so they are not only in harmony with life itself, and so ultimately alive, but at one with the entirety of their lives in a kind of harmonic perpetuity, which, if anything, resembles a spiritual physics, an awakening or a path to being awakened, whether we are aware of it or not of a spiritual continuum that can be accessed in our lives—which is what presence is.

Through the experience of presence, or finding the numinous in the commonplace, we are connected to all the moments of our lives. In practice, we certainly may not remember "the commonplace" Jack "can no longer remember," but it is, indeed, there—where Joseph Campbell, in discussion with Bill Moyers on the PBS television series *The Power of Myth*, describes a "higher consciousness" as being "right there, all the time." He further inflects that it is there close enough to reach out and touch, if it can be touched at all, which of course it is not actually able to be.

We don't have to miss immemorial breakfasts or our spouse, or partner, they are always with us, as are our beginnings and endings, the latter of which we may be prescient of or we may not know of at all; however, in our practice of presence we can enjoy the brilliant summer morning, we can be mindful of our driving onto the crushed black basalt driveway and to listen to the tires crackle over the stones. We can park the car in the barnyard where we saw the coyote only the other day, surprisingly just before noon, bounding into the thicket behind the cinderblock garage. We can step out of the car, breathing in the light breeze, and dig deep into our pockets for the keys to the studio where we will sit down to write, the studio erupting with the birdsong emitting through the screen door.

We are here in the moment, but we can also be connected to the first time we ever saw the studio, when our landlady opened it through the door from the mudroom, and we gasped as we saw the light shine on the planks of the yellow pine floor. These moments are linked and within our consciousness, through a kind of spiritual continuum, are a component of that presence, and are an active part of our own particular facet of now.

As with those two women perpetually standing on Waller Street in San Francisco, in Jack Gilbert's small but monumental poem, "Highlights and Interstices," whom are everlasting in the imagery he so masterfully conjures, and ironically and not without brevity, it is we, also, in our impermanence, who actually can veritably discover our eternity in the present moment any day and every moment all day. The practice of presence is a rigorous discipline, mostly because it is, indeed, a constant practice, and demands us to focus, to be mindful; and any such application can be exhausting, imprecise, and consuming. Most especially when we are exhausted it is difficult to practice, but it is also during these times when we become aware of the light flooding in through the cracks in our own armor, and because of our practice of presence an awakening may occur.

However, the key is in the practice itself, even in imperfect practice, since by sheer application of such practice of being conscious in the moment, we defy the odds and realize our birthright, which is the experience of finding the numinous in the commonplace, which then leads us to living the Christness of our lives in every moment of each day.

This includes the mindfulness of those two women on Waller Street, one of whom is lifting the child, as she is speaking with the other, and it is in that moment of "higher consciousness" and significant beauty in which we can reside no matter what the discussion or situation or event, and our lives become broadly multidimensional on a spiritual plane, since we are at one with our lives and in harmony within and beyond ourselves on levels and in ways heretofore unknown. These rich breakthroughs can occur each day if we are present. Similarly, as Joseph Campbell relayed, we just might be surprised into consequential amazement by such a practice — by locating the bliss in our living our lives, when he said "doors will open where you never believed that doors would be."

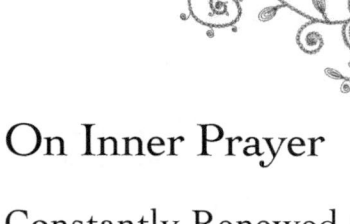

On Inner Prayer

Constantly Renewed Gifts

"*We must approach our meditation realizing that 'grace,' 'mercy,' and 'faith' are not permanent inalienable possessions which we gain by our efforts and retain as though by right, provided that we behave ourselves. They are CONSTANTLY RENEWED GIFTS. The life of grace in our hearts is renewed from moment to moment, directly and personally by God in his love for us.*"

—Thomas Merton, *Contemplative Prayer*

I REMEMBER READING THE SLENDER ANCHOR/ Doubleday paperback *Contemplative Prayer* by Thomas Merton, when I was twenty-two and searching for that tacit touchstone that might move me forward in the spiritual life. I remember reading Merton's substantive sentences, each one a log with which to keep warm on a winter's night, each one yielding heat in their cogency and direction. What I do not remember but just rediscovered is Merton's idea of "CONSTANTLY RENEWED GIFTS" in conjunction with prayer, since it is through prayer that we are sustained and it is by the renewal of prayer's gifts that we may live our lives more in harmony than in disharmony.

Before I came upon Merton and his enormous legacy as a writer and a poet, I was introduced to *The Way of a Pilgrim and The Pilgrim Continues His Way*, initially published in Russia in 1884. The book introduced to me what is known as "The Jesus Prayer," which is recited as, "Lord Jesus Christ, Son of God, have mercy on me, a sinner." Beginning in my commitment of reciting the prayer silently at the age of twenty, I have been devoted to the Jesus Prayer for nearly a half century. What I admired about the prayer was its intrinsic mantra-like nature—one that intersected with my Roman Catholic origins and my studies in Buddhism, as an active practioner of zazen with a small meditation group in the basement of Yale Divinity Chapel. The little prayer held resonance for a walker such as me, not unlike the Pilgrim, who walked blocks and blocks around campus finally having discovered a significant key toward spiritual practice.

I even used the prayer during my zen meditation practice in concentrating on my in-breath and out-breath, as in "Lord Jesus Christ, have mercy on me, a sinner." However, in later years, I dropped the last clause, and used the prayer in a more familiar fashion, leaving out spiritual judgment to God alone, and recited the prayer as, "Lord Jesus Christ, have mercy on me"—as I walked, hiked a mountain trail, stood in line at the grocery store, or even held my partner's hand. In conjunction to the latter, I often pray for those I love by inserting their name at the end of the prayer, instead of the second person pronoun. I also do this for friends who might be ill or in need. Just the idea of Cloistered Nuns, who pray for others all day every day has always been an inspiration for me; and although I am not a nun and will never become one, I do take delight in practicing inner prayer for others as much of every day and all day as I can. This practice centers my sense of presence and is a meditation that lends balance to my waking hours. It makes me think of a favorite poem by Federico Garcia Lorca, which I translated recently and reads:

Balanza

La noche quieta siempre.
El dia va y viene.

La noche muerta y alta.
El dia con un ala.

La noche sobre espejos
y el dia bajo el viento.

Balance

Night is quiet—always.
It is day that goes and comes.

Dead of night soaring.
Day with its wing.

Night hovering above mirrors,
And day stirring beneath the wind.

(*The Woven Tale Press*, Volume VIII, #6, Autumn 2020)

What inner prayer has done for me through each moment throughout the decades is that it has offered me a non-egoic point of practice through which I am constantly renewed. Especially in times of stress and even those stretches of chaos, through lean times, and during periods of dread, I have benefited, as well as those around me, by my practice of inner prayer. It is daily rigor, and by such rigor I have been broadened and deepened in and by simple spiritual practice. But what does this mean? Especially today during a pandemic and an economic crisis, during a Trumpian presidency of ineptitude and a country divided through malevolent means, what will inner prayer do or make any difference at all. Why bother to practice such a remote or even arcane exercise? Who will it benefit?

One answer is that inner prayer does, indeed, offer us, as Merton posits, constantly renewed gifts. It is through such renewal every day and all day that we redirect ourselves for our own sake and for the sake of others. We rechart our course through inner prayer—even though we may have an inner prayer practice it is through such practice and the consistency of it that we experience the beneficence of renewal. This is not a practice of entitlement but one of rigor. And, so, what is rigor and what is the difference between it and entitlement? Through rigor we attain practice and through practice we lose ourselves of what is egoic and that can be also attributed to the possessiveness of entitlement. Another book I think of often, which I read when I was twenty and then again when I was sixty, is Saint Theresa of Avila's *The Way of Perfection*. In it she writes of what I attempt to convey here:

> Therefore, sisters, have no fear that you will die of thirst on this road; you will never lack so much of the water of comfort that your thirst will be intolerable; so take my advice and do not tarry on the way, but strive like strong men until you die in the attempt, for you are here for nothing else than to strive.

It's that "striving like strong men" that has always sung to me. Since, as Saint Theresa writes and inflects lyrically, we "are here for nothing else than to strive." This is what true rigor and the rigor of practice is all about: an aim for consistency, an intent toward goodness. Yes, that last characteristic is, indeed, qualitatively subjective, since what is goodness; however, what it is, at least partially, is constantly renewing oneself through the practice and delight of inner prayer, which can be practiced anywhere, anytime, and any place.

What I hadn't mentioned is the benefit of practice itself, which can be sensual, as it is said Saint Theresa herself possessed similar proclivities, not dissimilar as D. H. Lawrence who also compared the life of the spirit to a kind of sensuality itself. There is an accompanying sweetness in practicing inner prayer—there is a dulcet nature about it. It is sublime and not fully ostensible, but it is present and it also makes us more present to our true nature. Dante's idea of *La Dolce Vita Nuova* (The Sweet New Life) is what's operative here. It is also reflected in Merton's postulation of constantly renewed gifts.

One of Joseph Campbell's great ideas regarding world mythology and religion is how he interprets the fourth chakra, or the heart chakra. Once, when asked about romantic love, Campbell uncharacteristically dodged the question, and relayed that Christ going out into "the marketplace of the world" was, indeed, what love was and what active loving was. That act, with the caveat of living from the heart chakra, which means living for others and for the benefit of others, is what we do when we, too, enter into "the marketplace of the world" in such a fashion by taking our monastic lives and our practice of inner prayer along with us among those we meet everyday all day. In a cogent way, we mask up so we can not only protect ourselves against Covid-19 but more importantly we also protect those whom we come into contact. By the practice of inner prayer, we mask up and actively lead a quiet and simple spiritual life by which we may wisely inflect goodness and grace on those we love and those we meet whom we may not love.

Such a practice as inner prayer, with its constantly renewed gifts, leads us toward an active humility, and it is through such an active humility that we can be receptive of grace itself.

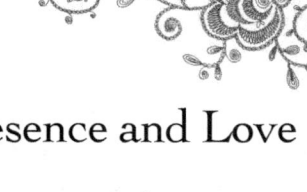

On Presence and Love

The Opening of the Heart

"The soul is made of love and must ever strive to return to love. Therefore, it can never find rest nor happiness in other things. It must lose itself in love. By its very nature it must seek God, who is love."

—Mechthild of Magdeburg

MY PARTNER ASKED ME SHORTLY AFTER THE first of the New Year the difference between the practice of presence and the act of loving. This happened to be in reference to a familial matter at hand and her questioning the actions of another in relation to both herself and her understanding of her feelings. Feelings aren't at all necessarily love, although love is often contingent on feelings. However, if one is hurt by someone, and what that person has said or done, especially without thoughtful consideration of that person's feelings, being present in experiencing those feelings can be pure anguish, and may even curtail the access to loving or even feeling love.

We often believe when we reach a certain age, at least the age when we can define ourselves in biological time as being an elder, that we might know enough to shield ourselves from our own insufferable natures and to rise above them. Furthermore, we often believe we can practice both presence and actively love when we experience moments of bliss: the Saturday morning concert at Tanglewood, finding the gem on the visit to the hospice shop, raising a fine glass of Cabernet to toast the blue cheese and mushroom omelet that you lovingly created, all those walks you enjoyed together, laughing in the sun. Those occasions become deeper when we are present and loving.

However, practicing presence, really staying with the moment, each and every moment, with mindfulness, is not easy. That is why it is a practice. We are given yet another opportunity to not only practice presence but also another chance at deepening and broadening our capacities to love. This, through such effort, further opens the heart in ways we are not privy to at once, but the heart does open more broadly and with more depth — not only in regard to our personal lives but for all those around us and everyone we meet.

We never know who we may affect. The medical intuitive Carolyn Myss recalls an anecdote about a young man who was so depressed that he had decided to board a city bus back to his apartment and commit suicide. A woman standing by the curb waiting for another bus looked up to the window where the young man was sitting, and smiled. She just smiled — in goodness, the goodness of the day, the goodness of life itself. This, the young man relayed to Myss, was the anecdote and panacea for him to not take his own life and to begin to live a newly inspired life altogether. The woman standing by the curb, waiting for her own bus to take her further into her own life, was not only practicing presence but was also offering her love. Granted, it was just a smile, but that smile bore what Eric Fromm may have called love for one's neighbor, even a young man whom she may not have been able to quite intuit was so depressed he had decided to take his own life. This woman was both present and loving, and the sheer power of this pairing can be incalculable.

However, what about being present and loving when someone has requested you do anything that may, momentarily, seem heartless. How do we manage to smile and bear such a psychological and psychic burden? How do we calculate the injury to our heart? Similarly, how do we practice presence through each moment, which can seem endless, during such a dilemma?

Actually, there is nothing other in such a situation than practicing presence and actively loving, as much as that can be difficult since both may seem inaccessible at the time. Also, inner prayer works. Inner prayer always works. It offers us substantively more than just our initial response to living through life's more difficult situations.

The Jesus Prayer ("Lord Jesus Christ, have mercy on me," which can also be amended to be prayed for another) provides nearly immediate nurture. Additionally, I am always reminded of the Holy Mother, especially when I am driving back to the studio from my partner's home since there is a statue of her, which then prompts me to begin to inwardly recite "Hail Marys" at least for the rest of the drive until reaching my destination.

Although what truly makes the most difference is mindfully

returning oneself to each and every moment, which constitutes the practice of presence. What constitutes such practice is staying present. It is not rehashing the past nor is it clouding what is called the future with the murkiness of thoughts, one way or another. Any mindfulness practice is work, and practicing presence is mindfulness practice. When we practice active spirituality on this level, we begin to notice a door open in the heart. No matter what anyone might have said or done to us largely falls away—or at least the pain of it does. What is replaced is the nascent glow of light within the heart. The warmth of the glow is what has been created through the spiritual alchemy of the practice of presence, and prayer, which is both active love, even from a distance, and the light of compassion, which is an outstanding guiding force—one that is healing, as well.

We live in a society that is ruled by outcomes: the outcome of an election; the decision of a judge; the final score of an athletic contest; whether or not, and even when, we might see our partner again, and under what circumstances. What we can come to terms with during any challenge or trial or duress is that the most opportune, and best, place we can find ourselves is in the moment. It is all we every have—by not really ever having it—since it is evanescent.

However, we also experience and observe that through being present in the moment we are able to realize our eternity, as much as that initially sounds overly intellectual it is also quite actively real. All those Saturday morning concerts in Tanglewood still exist. We can hear the orchestral beauty of the BSO. We can relive immemorial dinners and the sensuality of having walked and laughed in the sun. We may be alone in the world, which is certainly the case with our living in the duality of existence, but we can also feel connected to everything and everyone in the similar spiritual truth that all is one.

And, maybe, just maybe, we can begin to experience the light and warmth of the door swinging open in the heart, emanating both love and compassion, filling us and possibly lighting the way for those closest to us in our lives and in all of the lives of all those we may meet and even those we might not.

PART II

New Essays
and Reviews

Writer's Statement

On Beauty

MY PARTNER, TEVIS, DESCRIBED HER SEMI-
wakefulness this morning as her finding contentment
in her integrating the events of her life over the
past year and more as discovering that everything
fit together. The noted mythologist and expert of
comparative religion, Joseph Campbell, describes a
similar experience — during those times when we seem
to have an overview of our lives, when we view our
lives as a tapestry that has been woven together of
apparently disparate events but which we can now see
as exhibiting a pattern. This is beautiful.

Beauty is unique in that it can be seen in all of
its many facets. The 2015 film *The Fencer*, which
was nominated for a Golden Globe Award for Best
Foreign Language film and a Jussi Award for Best
Foreign Actor for Mart Avandi's fine performance in
portraying the story of Estonian fencer, Endel Nelis,
exhibits such beauty. It is a story, as all of our lives
are, of what Joseph Campbell terms the hero's journey.
There is beauty in this, too, since we all leave who we
once were and voyage out beyond ourselves, often in
a circular journey, whereupon we eventually return
home. However, return is never what we thought it
might be — since we have been changed by the journey,
even if those awaiting our return, as do the children
the fencing teacher coached and the woman he loved,
who steadfastly all waited for him, have changed,
before they meet him at the train station to welcome
his homecoming.

Homecomings are naturally beautiful. We leave
and return home daily. However, sometimes we return
back to ourselves to find that we have come through
either a dark night, with its intrinsic process of rebirth,

or through an entirely different type of process, if we have rigorously kept to whatever spiritual practices we may have maintained, and have been graced by either an awakening or even angelic visitation. Such experiences are only the beginning of seeing beauty in all of its many facets. Such experiences are often thought of as being ultimate and final encounters with the sacred and the divine; however, they truly indicate that these same experiences, which are, indeed, breakthroughs are limitless. There are as many opportunities to experience awakening and to be graced by visitations as there are stars in the sky.

Love and beauty are limitless. We can view the tapestry of our lives and begin to understand how we are connected to it as well as how that same tapestry is connected to the tapestry of everyone else. Our courage is not only to be exemplified by diminutive Marta, a student of Endel Nelis, who is pressed into competing with a much larger and older male fencer in the national fencing finals but also by Nelis himself who had an opportunity to escape but chose to lovingly coach Marta on the sidelines instead of opting for a false and empty freedom.

Considering our lives and seeing how all of what transpires in them fits while lying awake in the darkness before dawn is active grace. Moments such as these provide us with sustenance and nurture us. These moments are beautiful—as we return home either outwardly or within ourselves, especially when we find that we are filled incontrovertibly with a light that newly illuminates not only our own lives but also the lives of others we know and meet on the way.

Quiet Magnificence

Paul Chambers's Openings to Higher Consciousness, in a Limited Edition

DRY BONES IS PAUL CHAMBERS' THIRD BOOK of haiku poetry and it is published in a limited edition of only forty numbered and signed copies by The Red Ceilings Press of Derbyshire, Wales. What is made apparent in this aesthetically pleasing flat-spined paperback of new haiku by this Welsh haiku master, with its mesmerizing cover image, reminiscent of the paintings of Paul Klee, entitled "Chapel, Land and Sea," rendered by Adam David Taylor, is both its startling clarity and expansive largesse in its adept imagery.

However, stylistically, the collection is distinctively marked with asceticism. Although the collection includes a modest eighty-six haiku thoughtfully spaced amid fifty-six unnumbered pages, these haiku demand that the reader linger with each poem due to their surprisingly lasting resonance. Also, unlike most haiku collections that arrange the work by seasonal themes, *Dry Bones* is unique in its distinction of single page separations alerting the reader that there is a pause between groupings, which are more nuanced than any seasonal grouping.

The groupings are actually more actively psychologically nuanced, if not spiritually so. However, there is still a sense of season, since it is more unconsciously revealed, yet it is still deeply presented, so much so that the term *hosomi*, or lightness, can be applied here with these haiku. There is a kind of lightness in the layering of each haiku poem and then there is yet another connection in the juxtaposition of each haiku with each other. Additionally, there is a distinct sense of initially reading Shiki or Basho in English translation rather than reading any English-language haiku itself—since this work resonates so freshly as English-language poetry, which not all contemporary haiku written in English actually do.

What Paul Chambers accomplishes is capturing the lightning flash of the moment, as in the tensile imagery of "pylon hum/ the twitch of fibres/ in the horse's shoulder," or the cinematically etched images of "night bus . . ./ a handprint fills/ with moonlight." This is indicative of what Robert Spiess, former longtime editor of *Modern Haiku*, termed "felt-depth," which appears in striking abundance in Paul Chambers' work.

But also there is a nascent and active spirituality present within these haiku, deserving of a nod toward Thomas Merton, due to haiku such as "lichen/ in a stone angel's palm/ advancing rain," which connects us to what is sacred in what I term "finding the numinous in the commonplace." These haiku are not just haiku, they are poems that exhibit openings to higher consciousness, as in "convalescence . . ./ autumn revealing/ the river" or "pooling/ in a lemon rind/ evening rain."

The haiku of Paul Chambers, founding editor of *The Wales Haiku Journal*, is not only a haiku of self-awareness but it is also a poetry of cosmic awareness, exemplifying one's own mortality as well as one's own sense of eternity in the present moment, when he writes: "drizzling rain/ my reflection/ in the hearse." However, Paul Chambers can also be adequately described as a modern-day Issa too, when his vision so exquisitely portrays the suchness in seeing things just as they are, and releasing his readers on a journey of quiet magnificence: "sky clearing . . ./ a wren wipes its bill/ on a fence nail."

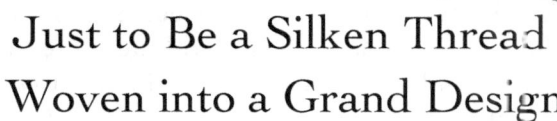

Just to Be a Silken Thread Woven into a Grand Design

Etudes: A Rilke Recital, Translations and Commentary by Art Beck (Shanti Arts, 2021)

> *"It's a need we have to lie together as*
> *delicately interwoven as petals and stamen.*
> *Until all the unbridled elements overflow*
> *everywhere and cover us in waves."*
>
> —Rainer Maria Rilke, from "Dawn Song,"
> translated by Art Beck

THE ANECDOTE OF JOSEPH CAMPBELL'S seems apt regarding my carrying Art Beck's *Etudes: A Rilke Recital* in my shoulder bag for some months, especially this second winter of Coronavirus, with Art Beck's Rilke translations acting as a beneficent constellation of guiding stars. When Campbell published his first book, which he co-authored with Henry Morton Robinson, *A Skeleton Key to Finnegan's Wake* (Harcourt, 1944), he commented that he had the distinct pleasure of having his wife, Jean Erdman, on one arm and a copy of *A Skeleton Key to Finnegan's Wake* under the other. During this second winter of Covid, I had the similar delight of having my partner, Tevis, on one arm and Art Beck's Rilke, literally, under the other.

I have often thought that we are quite fortunate to live in what I consider to be a golden age of translations. Translations of all sorts—and from all sorts of works of literature—have deepened our appreciation of every genre of literature. I recall first reading *Another*

Republic: 17 European and South American Writers (Ecco, 1976), edited by Mark Strand and Charles Simic, and intuitively come to know that doors opened to me that I didn't know were even there, to borrow a phrase from Joseph Campbell himself. Concurrent to my discovering such delight in the wealth of reading world literature in translations that were gloriously and aptly translated was the felicitous acquaintanceship with Stephen Mitchell, who was a graduate student at Yale at that time, and with whom I sometimes practiced zazen with, in a small group in the basement of Yale Divinity School Chapel. Stephen was then initially working on his own translations of Rainer Maria Rilke, and would quite often stop me as we passed in the street between classes, students sometimes streaming around us, to unlatch his brown briefcase with a golden metal latch and show me his newest translations, always neatly typed with a fresh black typewriter ribbon on a clean white page. Those moments, time and again, were gifts that he bestowed on me, explicating how difficult it was to capture the music of Rilke's German in our less than musical English. Now, nearly fifty years later, I am deeply delighted by another translator of Rilke whom I greatly admire, Art Beck, a longtime resident of San Francisco, who is the recipient of many accolades for his translations, including those of Luxorius, which won the 2013 Northern California Book Award for translated poetry, as well as an honorable mention in the American Literary Translators Association 2018 Cliff Becker Prize for his translations of Martial's epigrams.

It is significant in introducing the work of Art Beck, and especially that of his translations, since he is an accomplished poet in his own right, that he is both a literary purist and not just an intellect but an actively erudite intellect. I recommend reading Art Beck's essays in *Rattle* and the *Los Angeles Review of Books*. Few writers and thinkers exhibit any intellectual rigor these days. However, Art Beck does, and he does so with an unwavering humility, which also seems to be vacant from literary pretension and much writing in today's egoic discussions, reviews, and essays. In reading Art Beck, there is an ostensible sense of integrity — as well as freshness of vision and resonance in the written word itself.

Art Beck's *Etudes: A Rilke Recital* is a work of translation and insightful commentary that originated over the last forty years — finally culminating in his finishing the last dozen or so poems of Rilke's *The Sonnets to Orpheus* only in the last year or so. To hold such concretized life work between the covers of a reasonably thick book is a distinct pleasure, especially when it is as achieved as Art Beck's translations of Rilke. What makes these translations so accomplished, especially for those who have read Rilke in countless translations over the last half-century, is that they read with a crisp freshness, a sculpted line free of adverbs and adjectives, and a light touch in bringing what is probably one of the most mystical poetic sequences in all of twentieth-century literature, *The Sonnets to Orpheus*, into an English that is not only just highly readable but is liberated from the heavier-handed versions of Rilke, one of which Art Beck describes as sounding like "Pennsylvania Dutch." Art Beck's Rilke does seem, indeed, to be sculpted but even more distinctly as a stone cutter might split slabs of granite. Art Beck's Rilke reads in clean lines that snap like fresh white sheets in a spring wind. It is nothing less than refreshing to read a work such as *The Sonnets to Orpheus*, which can be so mystically inscrutable, and to finally begin to soar, as Rilke must have, in comprehending, and if not quite comprehending, then experiencing the mystical transformation of *The Sonnets to Orpheus* not only in song itself but also in taking the "risk" to actually become Orpheus, as Rilke writes, and Art Beck translates, in Sonnet XXIII, Second Part: "It's only fitting for us to keep praising,/ because, as it is, we're the branch and/ the axe and the sweet ripening risk."

Although Art Beck doesn't mention it, we, as readers, can nearly intuit and possibly feel Rilke going back and forth from the first desk that Nanny Wunderly-Volkart sent to him and then to the second, which she sent just in case the first never arrived, in composing the fifty-five sonnets that he wrote in the winter of 1923 in just a matter of two weeks. However, what Art Beck does make ostensible in his translations is an intimation of Rilke's clear sense of urgency and ebullience in the necessity to channel the work and to craft it, as an act of grace, written in a white heat, resonant for all time.

Initially, what makes Art Beck's translations of Rilke different from others is the quality of commentary that he introduces *Etudes* with and then with which he closes it. Parts of the commentary have appeared in such notable critical journals as *Jacket* and *Journal of Poetics Research*. Art Beck cites Scots poet Don Paterson's 2006 adaptation of Rilke's *The Sonnets to Orpheus*, and why his own work is a translation due to their "remain[ing] performances, perhaps, etudes of Rilke;" and that "they should be judged for their English, not for their German." He also delineates a brief time line of his own striving in translating Rilke in citing noted American poet and editor Dana Gioia publishing "a slim 1983 volume," edited by Gioia, entitled simply, *Rilke* (Elysium Press Poetry Series No. 5), in which a principle close to Art Beck's best as a translator remains *as*

performance doesn't preclude or qualify 'translation,' since "rather it helps to explain its possibility."

He continues that "translating poetry is writing poetry, but only harder." And this is where we hear Art Beck's humility speaking, whereas there are some translators who wear their hubris on their sleeves. He was aided by a grant from Centrum Arts in Port Townsend, Washington to translate *The Sonnets to Orpheus* back in 2004, and finished some fifteen years later in 2019, during which time he states, "I think I became not only a better reader of Rilke, but [also] a more technically adept poet. Both, I think, were the result of taking the time to internalize the poems, the way a pianist's fingers, say, absorb the spontaneity of the score through long repetitive practice."

The selection of poems that follow are primarily selected from Rilke's books *New Poems* (1907 and 1908), following his tenure as secretary to Rodin, which proved to be a formative experience for both poet and sculptor. These serve as a kind of list of not so much Rilke's better known poems but his most iconic, such as "Panther" and "Spanish Dancer," with "Panther" exhibiting both more of the animal's impatience as well as range within the close quarters of his cage, a rare agility within the never dying fires of the animal's wild eyes; and with the flamenco of "Spanish Dancer" going way past just the dance to enter into the *duende* of life itself well after the dance has ended and that essence resonating in the air. However, what Art Beck also includes here as a sort of Rilkean primer is a triptych of "Crucifixion/Resurrection" poems that bear more toward a Gnostic interpretation of Christ's death and His life after the crucifixion in such poems as "Crucifixion;" "Pieta" (1907), which belongs in this grouping of poems and which was inspired by Rodin's "Christ and the Magdelen,'" and "The Risen." Especially in "Pieta" (1907), we see the sensuality and spirituality Rilke exhibits so poignantly in these lines, with of course Magdelen speaking:

So it's like this, Jesus, I see your feet again.
They were a sweet stripling's feet then, when
I nervously undressed them to wash —
the way they stood confused in my hair
like a white deer caught in brambles.

Art Beck also connects Rilke's "Infant Apollo," which serves as a kind of first bookend in *New Poems (I)* and what is now one of Rilke's most famous poems "Archaic Torso of Apollo" that appears in *New Poems (II)*, in which as Art Beck points out in his commentary that closes *Etudes* that several eminent translators of Rilke, including

William Gass, Stephen Mitchell, M. D. Herter Norton, and Edward Snow have translated the *denouement* of the poem's final phrase similarly as "You must change your life" to what Art Beck nuances as "You have to live another life," which resonates quite differently philosophically, musically, and semantically.

This selection of Rilke's poems before both sets of the sonnets, which make up the bulk of *Etudes*, couldn't be referenced properly without mention of the poems "Beggars," "Corpse Washing," and "The First Elegy." In "Beggars," unlike Rilke's penchant for poems of praise, he creates a vignette in which "A stranger who/ stumbled on beggars peddling/ the palms of their hands there" also "spit as he tries/ to say something," almost as if this tableaux that is being exhibited is not only just a street scene but is also possibly Rilke's own fear expressed that his poetry may be rejected as too ethereal, which is further expressed in the lines, "his foreigner's face collapses/ right in front of their ruined eyes." "Corpse Washing" is another painterly poem forged in dark hues of the Dutch masters, as those tending to the menial task of cleaning the corpse are only shadows themselves and where "on the wallpaper/ their twisting shadows in a silent pattern/ flipped and flailed as if in a net."

However, a leap is detected from these masterful poems and their translations to "The First Elegy," written in 1912, the first of nine *Duino Elegies*, which presages WWI, and which Art Beck compares to T. S. Eliot's *The Wasteland*, that we begin to see Rilke building the brilliance of his true masterworks: both *Duino Elegies* and, in my mind, *The Sonnets to Orpheus*. It is impossible not to quote the entirety of the first verse of the Art Beck translation, since it is so seminal to Rilke's *oeuvre* and understanding him at all:

> Then even if I screamed to high heavens, who'd listen
> to me there among the angelic orders? And
> suppose one of them did swoop me to heart.
> I'd die, seared by exposure to that stark, concentrated
> being. Because beauty's nothing, the mere beginning
> of a panic we're still just barely able to contain.
> And we continually praise it, hoping it continues
> to disdainfully refrain from obliterating us.
> Every one of the angels is horrifying.

What makes Art Beck's translation of "The First Elegy" not only different but quite separate from some of the better translations of it, such as the one by William Gass, is that Art Beck relays in his commentary that he is "tempted to take that wry intimate voice farther in English, bordering on idiom." He explicates further in his wanting to craft poems and not only representations of them: "Above all they seem to lack the element of risk that—like flight—poetic translation demands." What makes Art Beck's translations not only different but quite separate is not only this aspect of his risk-taking for the sake of "flight" that poetic translation may demand but also his predilection for perfection as he relays in an anecdote about his finding a tattered Hachette German-English dictionary at a garage sale in San Francisco, published circa 1910, about the time Rilke may have been finishing "Archaic Torso of Apollo," and Art Beck's rumination of the definition for *Kandelaber*, which is "chandelier." In several former translations he cites there are other words used for *Kandelaber*, but he makes his choice as "chandelier," and as we observe how this illumines the poem in quite another way, never mind making for a more apt assonance and alliteration in English: "But his torso/ still stares like a chandelier turned low,/ dimmed to illuminate just its own steady/ flame."

However, as significant as these translations of Rilke are they are significant because of the achievement of their sere, yet compliant, translations of *The Sonnets to Orpheus*. These are nonpareil. We can read other translations by other adept translators but it is in Art Beck's sonnets we can see more clearly than in any other the tree growing out of Orpheus's ear, and "a temple of resonance/ in their deepest hearing, a refuge of darkest desire,/ and entrance of trembling door posts" like no other translation I've read before. Perhaps it is in Art Beck's own words we can plumb not only the intent of his translation but also the depth of his understanding of Rilke's very ethos and the composition of these fifty-five sonnets he didn't even expect to write; yet after having written *Duino Elegies*, a much protracted sequence having taken over a decade to complete, Rilke's creative floodgates opened fully. As Art Beck extrapolates about *The Sonnets to Orpheus*:

> [They] are rich with death, but imbued with Rilke's own demise, still unaware of that weight about to fall. For Rilke in the Sonnets, death and the dead seem like deep bass notes from an organ preparing to soar... Not the rumbling of a pitiless volcano . . . but the Minotaur's cold breath.

These sonnets are, eminently, rich in life too. Dedicated to a girl Rilke's daughter, Ruth, knew, named Vera Knoop, a former dancer who died tragically at a young age, these sonnets exhibit a kind of sonic dimensionality unto themselves, and in Art Beck's translation, they do, indeed, soar as he makes reference to in his introductory notes, much like the rising octaves of an organ's bass notes.

What is also apparent is that especially in Art Beck's translations of *The Sonnets to Orpheus* there is a clarity within a clarity in that what becomes clear, besides the Orphic song registering through Rilke and in Art Beck's English, is that in Part I, Orpheus is presented and alluded to in all of his glory, whereas in Part II we can observe, and hear, Rilke's metamorphoses in Orpheus, and by the end of the sonnet sequence, it is Rilke who becomes Orpheus. Moreover, it is my own interpretation of rereading this translation that we, as readers, also are given our own Orphic lift in staying the course with Rilke through this transporting journey in *The Sonnets to Orpheus* — not that we become God-like in the Nietzschean sense but we are brought about, in more of a Jungian concept, closer to our archetypal origins of elemental song.

What does this mean? If we are to follow some of the more radiant sonnets, VII, Part I we can discover Rilke's credo expressing praise as one of the better forms of poetry, as well as in life. Rilke is clear, as Art Beck's translation is as fresh as a bucket of water drawn up from the depths of a well:

That's what it's all about: Praise and all its glory.
From one who's on a mission of praise, glittering
like ore in the mute stone. His humanity
a mortal grape press, squeezing out the eternal wine.

Praise for Rilke is not anything that occludes the reality that our lives are riven also with the depths of sorrow and grief. In VIII, Part I, this sonnet is so perennially fresh that immemorial dew still remains on the images themselves and that lightness exhibits a feeling as if we could magically enter a holograph, and exist there, momentarily. Art Beck's inflection also presents a knowing touch.

Jubilation knows, and Longing's already confessed.
Only Grief 's still learning her role.
All night she enumerates the ancient wrongs

on girlish fingers. Yet suddenly, surprised
and raw, a constellation of our voices leaps
out of her into the sky untouched by her breath.

What also makes Art Beck's translations of *The Sonnets to Orpheus* both different and separate from any other, and very possibly due to the clarity that signifies these translations, is the connection between each sonnet and their own tintinnabulation that resonates among themselves. An example of this is in considering the last two sonnets of Part I. With Rilke writing possibly up to four or more sonnets per day over a two-week period, and perhaps changing from one desk to another, even depending upon the sunlight slanting in one way or in an alternative direction, Rilke not only characterizes Orpheus as heroic but also in concluding Part I intimates our own heroism in these lines from XXV and then in XXVI, which also points particularly toward transcendence:

> Again and again the intervals of darkness and ruin returned
> Your blood slickened with earth and pounded like a hammer.
> The door hopelessly opened — and you entered.
> [XXV]

> Forsaken god. Eternal echo and scent. Only
> because of the hate that rent and scattered you
> does nature have a voice that speaks with us.
> [XXVI]

If *The Sonnets to Orpheus*, Part I can be thought of as a kind of descent into song then Part II is not only the ascent of song but also its example of one aria after another. And this is true enough that it is not only song but it is dance too:

> Breath you imperceptible poem!
> Constantly pulling our splintered existence
> into genuine commerce with the universe.
> Counterpoint whose dance I rhythmically become.

Herein, Rilke begins his own Orphic transformation, as do we. This occurs openly and in a similar and surprisingly Whitmanesque voice. The organic ontological musing here is not without its ascendant arc and not without its apparent realization. However, we've only just begun Part II, and we enter depth after depth as we enter aria after aria. In III, Part II, "mirrors" become prescient of what filmmaker Jacques Cocteau would recreate in his classic *La Belle et la Bette* (*The Beauty and the Beast*), 1946:

> Mirrors — no one has ever been able to really guess
> who you are when you're alone with yourselves:

When the spaces between time sift
like water through your sieve.

In XI, Part II, Rilke conjures his own iconic image of the rose,
and his intended eternal nature, as well as providing rather stunning
imagery evocative of "the etheric body.' This, indeed, is Rilke being
Rilke; however, it is also Art Beck skillfully translating Rilke, not
under-translating him or over-translating, not making him more
mystical or less mystical, but in an almost secular fashion translating
Rilke as he is, in his essence, which allows a light, albeit a mystical
light, shine through the interstices of the images themselves, even the
"costumes" of the ego:

Enthroned rose: In the old days
you were a chalice with a simple brim.
But, now—you've fully bloomed for us,
an infinitely, inexhaustible subject.
In your richness you're like cloak upon
cloak covering a body of nothing but
light. All the while each individual petal
eludes and disdains all costumes.

Possibly what is the most inscrutable but yielding to
understanding of all of *The Sonnets to Orpheus*, as well as so
immemorially Rilkean, even inexhaustibly so is XIII, Part II, which
begins "Anticipate each goodbye as if it were/ already behind you
like a winter that's passed./ Because underneath these winters is
such an interminable/ winter, that only by hibernating can your
heart survive." However, it is in the conclusion of this sonnet that
we find Rilke, as well as Art Beck, plumbing depths few poets or
their translators ever discover new meaning with each rereading:
"To those already used and discarded/ and to the numb, mute/
stockyard of bloated nature—to that unspeakable sum—/ count
yourself gladly in and nullify the count.' The psycho-spiritual
counterpoint here is that we accept life fully in living life fully, and
in that we reach a kind of apotheosis in which we let go of it and
give way to living it concomitantly.

This notion is expressed differently in XXI, Part II, and is
reminiscent of Jack Gilbert's opening poem in *Refusing Heaven* (Knopf,
2005), entitled "A Brief for the Defense," in which he concludes: "To
hear the faint sound of oars in the silence as a rowboat/ comes slowly
out and then goes back is truly worth/ all the years of sorrow that are
to come." Although in Art Beck's *Etudes*, we have Rilke reiterating

a theme of giving yourself up to become one, to become not only Orpheus but Orphic, to become one with everything:

> Resist the illusion of privation. Let yourself
> accede to that longed for decision: Just be!
> A silken thread woven into the grand design.
> Whatever image in it calls you (even if it's
> just a moment in a lifetime of grief), feel
> how the whole glorious carpet is implicit.

Even more simply than becoming one with everything, through Rilke's observation we can become aware what Joseph Campbell intimated—that in looking back upon your life, in times of self-assessment and in rumination, you can observe the wholeness of it, the holistic nature of each thread having woven itself immeasurably among all the others to have become an entity unto itself.

For *The Sonnets to Orpheus* to come full circle is no surprise with such a lyrical masterwork, however, for it to honor, once again, Vera Knoop, the young dancer, is a preeminent conclusion, a finale of consequence—and, of course, the message of the final two sonnets, and of the entire sequence, itself: transcendence. We can't help but notice how the ending of both the penultimate sonnet and the final one resonate and are in harmony with one another.

> . . . But you
> still danced to that once-upon-a-time,
> even a little bit annoyed if a tree seemed
> slow to attend your impatient ear.
> You always understood the lyre's
> resonant source—its outrageous heart.
> And so you rehearsed lovely steps
> hoping to one day guide your friend's
> attention to this healing celebration.
> [XXVIII, Part II]

> . . . At the crossroads of this overwhelming
> night be the sorcerer and spell, the catalysts
> of your being's uncanny convergence.
> And if what's earthly forgets you,
> remind the silent earth: I flow.
> Tell the hurrying water: I am.
> [XXIX, Part II]

❧

Distinguished writer and critic Marjorie Perloff is quoted by Art Beck in his commentary in closing *Etudes* in suggesting that Rilke's voice in *Duino Elegies* "remains conversational and contemporary, unlike the highly mannered 'high poetic' tone of many of the translations." With this adroit speculation, and in giving consideration to Art Beck's translations of Rilke in *Etudes*, we clearly see how Art Beck's Rilke actually becomes achievements unto themselves, since besides their uncanny but hard-won crispness, they attain conversational and contemporary lyricism—in English.

In writing about "The First Elegy," Art Beck contemplates, "I've always felt that Rilke stands with one foot in the nineteenth-century and the other planted in the twenty-first. I've sometimes thought of him, especially in *The Elegies* as the poetic leg of a three-legged stool— the other two being Einstein and Freud/Jung."

If Rilke is then one of three poetic legs of such a stool that it is the glue and artistry that Art Beck represents in making Rilke's writing, particularly *The Sonnets to Orpheus*, poetry that is providentially resilient and substantive that it should be sturdy enough to hold firmly with Einstein and Freud/Jung. Of the many translations of Rilke, Art Beck's work, which is the effort of nearly fifty years, is abundant in its accomplishment. In its accomplishment, there is a keen sense of achieving a translation that resonates within itself but also resounds among other writers of formidable talent and message, such as Art Beck's translation of XXV, Part II, in which there is an almost ghostly tinge of a Georg Trakl-like timbre, which is also similar in tone and image, but clearly Rilkean itself, as Rilke lavishes praises on "what always captured you," but it is with his patent sense of the tranquil within transcendence that he, and Art Beck, can see, hear, and inhale in this world, and as secular as Art Beck can be in his pursuit of the extraordinary amid the ordinary, we are presented with yet another immemorial vision in the timelessness of the ever-present.

> Tonight, even the budding leaves of
> wintered oaks glow in an olive dusk.
> Soft gusts whisper and nod. The shrubs
> are still black, but heaped fertilizer spreads
> its richer black across the open land. Every
> hour that passes grows younger.

To Be Both Body and Spirit

The Angled Road: Collected Poems,
1970–2020 by Jonas Zdanys,
Lamar University Press, 2020

TOWARDS THE END OF HIS WATERSHED BOOK, *The Angled Road: Collected Poems, 1970-2020,* Jonas Zdanys writes in the poem, "Love," that "Our lives" are "a vigil/ for something whiter/ than snow," which represents Zdanys as a reverential poet, one whose reverence is that of the harmony of the intellect and the heart (as in the compassion exhibited in the fourth chakra). These lines also portray his penchant for an economical poetry, and may be evidence of his having studied with the late Robert Creeley who was master of the tightness of phrase while still instilling an active and poignant lyricism in his poetry. However much may be due to Creeley's influence, Zdanys is not only a poet of significance but is also largely his own poet. What he follows the lines quoted above is solely his own creation and why that is important is because Zdanys writes memorable verse: "Now, words are dry,/ like seagull footprints/ in the sand,/ sweepings, dust.// Bitter you say,/ the world's beginning./ You laugh when I say/ how beautiful it was."

Zdanys's *Collected Poems* is his fiftieth book and gathers fifty years of his poetry. That level of a poetic canon includes his many translations from his native Lithuanian many of which are considered contemporary classics for their singular achievement of the mastery of translations alone, such as *Five Lithuanian Women Poets* (Vilnius: Vaga Publishers Ltd., 2002), which has earned him recognition and respect internationally. However, as much as Zdanys will be remembered as a translator, he will be remembered so only because of his aesthetic and intellectual abilities as an American poet.

It is observed that Zdanys implementing "a modern, multidimensional chaotic consciousness" to his translations of Lithuanian language poetry but it also concomitantly "reinforces a conservative humanistic agenda"—and that is quite a juxtaposition of literary descriptions. What this is indicative of is that this enjambment of "multidimensional consciousness" and a "conservative humanistic agenda" may be an apt overall description of what forces are operative in the alchemy of Zdanys's marriage of intellect and lyricism in his own poetry.

Zdanys is a practiced gardener in the fields of literature for more than a half century. He writes in "October Garden" that "Like all gardeners, I am bound to the patch/ of dirt I cultivate and to the seeds I plant,/ each a universe of labor and each/ a point in the tally of the passing days." The rhythm in these lines is both harmonic in its lyricism and sonic in its metaphysical exegesis of our circadian ontological existence itself. What is ostensible here is that Zdanys is a poet of ideas, and is a cerebral poet, but nearly magically he is able to craft such perennial philosophy into the interplay of song—and to do so in such an unobtrusive manner that we as readers are deceived by his light and sure touch. Zdanys continues in such a manner in this poem in such a way and mesmerizes us without our barely noticing it:

Time bears everything onward and forward
in its flow and there is in fact now
little left to do, only to gather stray leaves
from time to time and turn them over
into the earth, listen to the silence
that drops across the garden when the wind
in the trees unexpectedly stops,
record the changes of the moon.
It is possible in this way to be both
body and spirit, to know that there will be
another summer in which to try again,
another time to be sure the seed does not die out.

"To be both/ body and spirit" is essential Jonas Zdanys. His "October Garden" is not just a paean to the finality of the autumn season but is also at the same time a realization of the resurrection within us and quite significantly of the matrix of our being "body" and "spirit," which as subtle as this might seem is what a true awakening is.

Undoubtedly, there is *mysterium tremendum* present in this poem, but that is presented in a way that is as light as a feather—and that is what mesmerizes us as readers. Zdanys as poetic metaphysician displays his own arcs and angles, in The *Angled Road: Collected Poems*

1970–2020, through the craft of the poem, which can be likened to a cosmic compass of his own creative invention. Although Zdanys doesn't mention or directly allude to any names, what he is inculcating in this matrix of "body" and "spirit" is essential "Christness" or inherent Buddhism, indeed, any activated intrinsic spirituality that defies definition due to its abandonment of any rhetorical device except for the very images in the poem itself and the transparency of the lyricism that carries those images, which then leaves us as we are, momentarily enlightened, in the lines of Zdanys's "October Garden."

Another example of Zdanys's reverence for what is poetically refined and through that refinement his predilection for not so much framing the metaphysical in his poems but in releasing it through the lyricism of them is found in third section of his poem, "Bones:"

When I touch you, stars fall,
gather together dry and dead in your hair.

When you touch me, clouds
lift and tremble, burst into seed and flame.

Yesterday is a scattering of broken twigs
near the fence of an old house.

Today is a ragged sigh of a soul
measuring its loses in a burling wind.

Tomorrow is desire, heavy with sorrow,
a bone with wings brittle at both ends.

Such a poem summons the work of Czech poet and immunologist Miroslav Holub who often made use of his medical knowledge to effect his poetry but, again, Zdanys has a conception of the world stage with regard to literary achievement and he makes a viable statement in this poem for his standing among the best in treading the boards along that platform and dais. Besides, how many poets would use the verb "burling" in such a way and with such utter confidence? Who else but perhaps the surrealist French poet Andre Breton might even write "a bone with wings," especially one "at both ends?" Zdanys's deep Euro-American roots gleam with a rich poetic loam, out of which sprout metaphor *magnifique*.

Another characteristic of Zdanys is his infusing a kind of disciplined magical surrealism, which is somewhat of an oxymoron, found, for instance, in the poetical prose of Bruno Schulz, from his books *The Street of Crocodiles* or *Sanatorium Under the Sign of the Hourglass*, or in the poetry of other Polish poets, such as Nobel Laureate Wislawa Szymborska, or poet/playwright Tadeusz Rozewicz. The first section of the opening poem in Zdanys's book *The Thin Light of Winter*, entitled "In the Land of Blue Shadow" is a real treat to read and is emblematic of the best of Zdanys. The poem is attributed to being written "after" Henrikas Nagys. Again, we as readers are mesmerized and transported by its entrancing rhythms and rich imagery, which are interwoven into a poetic spell that Zdanys casts upon the page, which takes us places beyond us and out of ourselves, which is the mark of any accomplished writing of any kind.

> We trace the child's face in the first snow.
> My sister sleeps under wild raspberry branches.
> Last night workmen spread light snow
> on frozen ground white as my mother's hair.
>
> We trace my brother's face in the first snow.
> the guard's epileptic daughter crumbles
> dry bread on the echoing ground.
> We hear it falling as the wild clouds bleed.
>
> Birds shrug moonlight from their frozen backs.
> Beneath the ice rivers flow slowly to the sea.
> My sister's doll sleeps under wild raspberry branches.
> We trace my brother's cold face in the snow.

This poem also resonates with echoes of Miklos Radnoti's *The Clouded Sky*, which was a manuscript of poems found by his wife in the Hungarian poet's coat pockets in a mass grave at the end of World War II after an ill-fated forced march commandeered by the Nazis of the survivors of a concentration camp in which Radnoti had been held prisoner. Similarly, Zdanys's parents had been held in a concentration camp in Lithuania before they immigrated to this country and made their home in New Britain, Connecticut, where Zdanys was born in 1950.

Most fortunately, Zdanys's parents survived their travails after being in a United Nations camp for Lithuanian refugees, and what survives in Zdanys is the song of survival, the lyricism of a poetry so original in its craft that through the force of its very words we discover that we are, indeed, both body and spirit. The poetry of Jonas Zdanys is one of a rich poetic heritage and one in which he endows to us in perpetuity his supreme reverence for not only the intellect but the resonance of scrupulously milled words that he has refined into the nourishing bread of song.

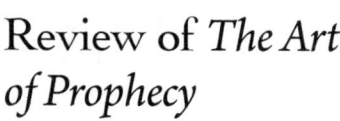

Review of *The Art of Prophecy*

A How-To Guide from Beyond the Grave
by Amos, a Major Minor Prophet by David
Breeden, Wipf and Stock/Cascade, 2020

IT IS APT THAT ONE OF THE SEVERAL QUOTES from a variety of notable authors prefacing David Breeden's *The Art of Prophecy: A How-To Guide from Beyond the Grave by Amos, a Major Minor Prophet* would include the French philosopher Alain Badiou, a colleague of Gilles Deleuze and Michael Foucault, who writes about such concepts as truth not being either postmodern or a simple repetition of the concept of modernity, and whose philosophy just may be expressed succinctly by the quote used here, "Justice does not exist, which is why we must create it." A minor prophet from the Bible, Amos was an eight century BCE shepherd and dresser of sycamore trees, who was discerning enough to point up the differences of the ruling elite and take issue with it.

It is Amos to whom Breeden gives voice in poems that are reminiscent of William Carlos Williams, written in American idiom, as well as epistolary prose poems that conjure the work of Russell Edson. However, David Breeden's poetry is refreshingly his own, as in these lines from the poem "A Resume from the Other End of the Spectrum" in which Amos concretizes his criticism of the upper class, "Thataway, where the fattest parasites/ themselves. Where the high/ 'n mighty sat, attached, sucking// our blood. Thataway where a new/ Pharaoh always sits, looking to lion/ us all up like so many lamed// sheep." Lines such as these are also evocative of Edward

Dorn's persona poems in his book *Gunslinger*, considered to be one of the best long poems of the 1960s.

And as Breeden has Amos himself quoting Foucault, we as readers sit up straighter so we can best listen to the depths of truth found in these poems, "Truth is a thing of this world, produced only by virtue of multiple forms of constraint." But as Breeden may know Badiou and Foucault, he knows his own soul and the soul of man when he writes so eloquently of the spiritual rigors of silence, "As I said, the one thing you learn in the desert night is silence. You develop one of those intimate relationships with silence. Roaring, deafening silence. Makes some tell stories. Makes some sing songs. Makes some hear things."

Breeden, who has also adapted Laozi's *Daodejing* (Lamar University Press, 2015), includes Verse 23 from this Eastern classic in this book, and offers much wisdom here in these lines, "When we make The Way our study/ Those attempting to practice it/ Agree with us, and those attempting/ To pursue it agree with us, and/ Even those failing to attempt it// Agree with us.// But when we stop/ Our own attempts/ All others lose faith in us." What Breeden is illustrating through Laozi is the spiritual law that we are not only all connected, and ostensibly all One, but not unlike the concept of *Antahkarana*, developed by Elizabeth Claire Prophet, which is essentially "the web of life" or specifically "the net of light spanning Spirit and Matter connecting and sensitizing the whole of creation within itself and to the heart of God." What Breeden posits is that it us on us and within us—all our acts and thoughts and how we focus our will is our largest asset and our most formidable strength, that everything counts, and as the prolific Native American poet Carroll Arnett, or *Gogisgi*, once Chief of the Overhill Band of the Cherokee Nations, once wrote, "Everything counts/ and nothing happens fast."

Breeden also makes use of a kind of dialect that made the *Pogo* comic strip popular and vivid, as in the eponymous character's well-known phrase, "we have met the enemy and he is us." This kind of American patois works to portray Joan of Arc and make her contemporary, "Ask Sister Joan D'Arc, speaking of *par examples* and the peasantry and all. She'll tell you: Getting to the place of speaking truth is a costly little process. Your whole darn dirt-poor domestic servant gene pool is going to add up to the truth you tell. and when you're comin' from there, ain't nobody gonna listen. You're gonna get yer bum fried."

Another example of this use of dialect, which appears throughout the book, is when Amos is speaking lyrically about truth, both then and now, since these are notes to us from the other side, and Breeden's poetry is poignant, even unfortunately timeless:

Sycamore pruner.
Makes me sound like I was out
in somebody's garden trimming
trees for an extra buck.

No. Out in the hedgerows
cutting the damnedest
poorest excuse for a fig-like
something that there is.

Just to sell something to
poor folks so that they feel
like they've eaten something
like the rich folks, who buy
figs as an afterthought.

Also, *Confessions of a Minor Prophet* is not without virtuoso
imagistic turns, such as the following example, from "Thanks for Asking
(a rantette)," with Amos once again soliloquizing: "That I was all kinds
of ersatz and cardboard back in my carbon-based days. Admit it. That's
what you think . . . . A shadow play in a cardboard factory."

Actually, Breeden develops what can be termed a doxological
lyricism in this book-length poem that is also dialectical and intrinsic to
an ontological phenomenology in which he constructs a language that is
both poetical and metaphysical at once, and perhaps in doing so paying
homage to both Martin Heidegger and Gaston Bachelard, as in these lines
from "The Primate Paradox," which are some of the best lines in the book:

Any word contains
other words in its
meaning and is
only part of
a system of words.

For every action
there is the choice;
there is the action;
then there is
the interpretation.

Every emotion has
a story, a history.

Human beings cannot act
outside of human nature —
all human actions
are human nature.

There is also a palpable echo of D. A. Levy, whom Gary Snyder fashioned an entire essay about in his book, *The Old Ways* (New Directions, 1977). The essay regarding this little known Cleveland poet who flourished in the mid-1960s is entitled "The Dharma Eye of D. A. Levy," and Breeden exercises his own "dharma eye" in a poem such as "I See You," which additionally reveals one of the richer veins in a work that is significant to look at both as a whole and in part due to its containing a number of sparkling gems — as did the *oeuvre* of D. A. Levy as is indicated by Gary Snyder in his essay.

Look, the days are coming, YHWH says,
when the plowman shall overtake the reaper,

and the treader of grapes the sower;
and the mountains will drop sweet wine,
and all the hills will melt.

and I will bring my people of Israel out of captivity,
and they will rebuild the wasted cities and inhabit them;

and they will plant vineyards,
and drink the wine from them;

they shall also make gardens,
and eat the fruit from them.

I shall plant them upon their land,
and they shall be pulled up no more
out of their land
which I have given them,

YHWH says so.

David Breeden makes his book-length persona poem about Amos a work of visionary and prophetic beneficence — perhaps worthy of the announcement of a newly amended New Testament.

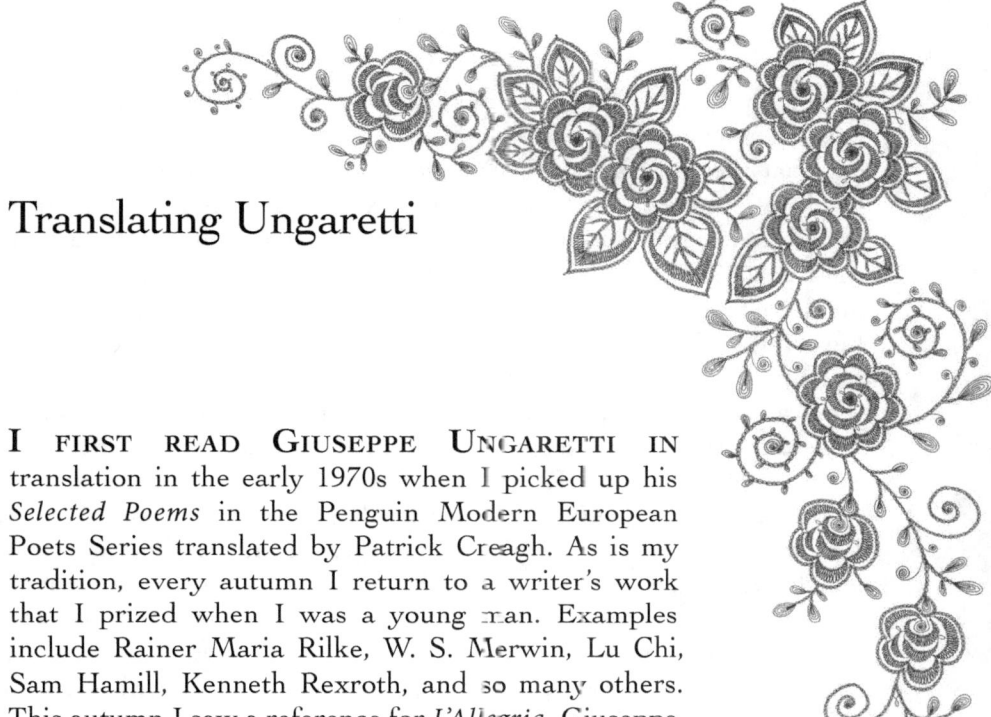

Translating Ungaretti

I FIRST READ GIUSEPPE UNGARETTI IN translation in the early 1970s when I picked up his *Selected Poems* in the Penguin Modern European Poets Series translated by Patrick Creagh. As is my tradition, every autumn I return to a writer's work that I prized when I was a young man. Examples include Rainer Maria Rilke, W. S. Merwin, Lu Chi, Sam Hamill, Kenneth Rexroth, and so many others. This autumn I saw a reference for *L'Allegria*, Giuseppe Ungaretti's first book of poems written in the mud-spattered trenches of World War I, and I intuited deeply that it would be Ungaretti that I would be turning to during the sere days of the season of colored leaves, windstorms, and rain.

However, when I went to my local library to check out the volume, upon walking to the parking lot to my car, I found that the book was a 1942 edition of *L'Allegria*, and it wasn't dual language, as I had surmised, but it was the Italian edition published by Arnoldo Mondadori Editore. It is a beautiful little medium octavo 8- by 5-inch edition that fits nicely in the hand, as I used to describe books such as this dimension as both a new, used, and antiquarian bookdealer that I was for several decades now many years ago. Although I was initially bemused by my miscalculation about my borrowing this edition from the library, and integrating my mistake of taking out a book in Italian I couldn't necessarily read, the voice of my guide came rising up and through me in providing the guidance that I should actually translate the book line by line and poem by poem. The guidance instantaneously became my resolve.

I had long admired Denise Levertov for many

reasons but one of those reasons was that she translated the French poet Eugene Guilevic (1907–1997) without having known French; and that she had translated his poetry line by line by using a French-English dictionary. Perhaps Denise Levertov gave me the necessary inspiration to solidify the direction of my guidance, since I undertook the translation of *L'Allegria* in a similar fashion, although I developed my initial translations using online references. Essentially, as did Levertov with Guilevic, I turned the direct translation of Ungaretti into modern American poetry.

Translating Ungaretti is not as easy as it might appear. Although largely short poems, except for the longer and often more complex poems such as "*I fiumi*/Rivers" and "*Giugno*/June" for instance, it is not the length of any poem by Ungaretti that proves a challenge. Rather, it is the modernist nuances of his language, the practiced hermeticism, which originated in the work of Hermes Trismegistus, and which the fourteenth century Italian scholar Marcelo Ficino translated and espoused, as being, simply, that the universe is based upon "cosmic vibrations in the substance of the All." However, Ungaretti was also influenced by the Dadaist movement, and poets he had met in Paris before the war, such as Romanian poet Tristan Tzara, and Ungaretti's poetry can also be categorized as being symbolist in character. Ungaretti paints miniatures, even in his longer poems by successfully pasting in one scene after another, as in "*Transfigurazione*/Transformation," not unlike the pointillist painters such as Georges Seurat and Camille Pissarro, created their images on canvas. Ungaretti's style can be described as all of this but also he is an imagist, and it was through his images that he initially attracted me as a young writer and continues to earn my respect and admiration.

I remember reading Patrick Creagh's translations in the Penguin Modern European Poets Series, edited by A. Alvarez, on my lunch breaks from the bookstore I worked in, Book World, on Chapel Street next to the Yale Art and Architecture Building, for some months, carefully rereading each poem, turning over each image in my mind, in the same way I might cherish a clear glass marble in my hand. Eventually, I would go on to write short poems after Ungaretti that would be published in *Rolling Stone*, although imitating his characteristic deep image I would never achieve his aesthetic mastery of hermeticism or symbolism, although I would continue to practice imagism for the entirety of my life as a writer.

After finishing my translation of *L'Allegria*, I discovered that there is another translation of the work recently published. Although initially disconcerting, since I thought I might be resuscitating Ungaretti's reputation, especially with this iconic first book of poetry that glimmers with "cosmic vibrations" of sunrises and meadows in depicting deep moments of the sublime but also the harrowing moments of war, since there are previous translations from this book in selections of Ungaretti published in both 1975 and 2002, however, I am grateful I listened to the guidance that directed me to create my own translations of the work — just for the sake of the rigor and the depth of experience of getting as immeasurably close to not only Ungaretti's poetics but to his life as he led it, and its many vicissitudes, during the years of WWI from 1914 through 1919.

What I observed myself doing in translating Ungaretti was, often enough, providing a different, and I believe most optimal, syntactical translation of his work in comparison to some of the other extant translations. Also, I believe my verb choice, as an imagist poet (which is evident even in my short narrative poems) of a more specific verb, such as in "*Un Sogno Solito*/A Habitual Dream," in which I use the verb "sequined" in describing how the water of the Nile dressed the women Ungaretti witnessed standing along the banks after their swimming in the river. Some of these translations can only truly be rendered in a line by line direct translation from the Italian; most others need the interpretive and poetic verve in representing their meaning in English and significantly in the parlance of modern American poetry, as much as that parlance is of my own voice and my own making. So, it is my belief, and positive intentionality, that these translations that I offer of Ungaretti are not only different from any other but they are also of at least a modicum of importance and that they have a life of their own in their being a creation unto themselves and of their own.

With this stated, my own imperative in translating Ungaretti has been to impart Ungaretti to any reader — to attempt to instill the apparent *sprezzatura*, or "studied carelessness" with a touch of *elan*, which is characteristic of Ungaretti's poetry, but also the *scintillante*, or the *sparkling* element, and a phrase I use often in translating Ungaretti, crystalline expression, that he instills and is a compelling agent in the nature of his work.

I have previously made some translations of Rainer Maria Rilke, Georg Trakl, Juan Ramon Jimenez, Saint John of the Cross, and Federico Garcia Lorca — publishing several of these; however, this is my first full-length book of translations. It is my positive intentionality that this is also my sharing of my love and ardor for the poetry of Giuseppe Ungaretti, and most especially, his *L'Allegria*, his *Cheerfulness* in the face of adversity, and through that adversity his discovery of the serene.

I am grateful for this opportunity of translating Ungaretti and of having listened to the guidance that I heard. May these translations of Ungaretti sing to you as Ungaretti has clearly sung to me, as in the final poem in this collection, "Prayer."

Prayer

Parigi—Milano 1919

When I awake
from inflamed profligacy
within a crystalline, astonished space

When my weight becomes light once again

The shipwreck endows me, Lord
the first exclamation of a new day

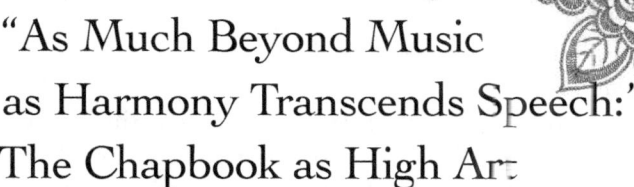

"As Much Beyond Music as Harmony Transcends Speech:" The Chapbook as High Art

The Insistent Island by Art Beck

I FIRST CAME ACROSS THE POETRY OF ART Beck while working as a cataloguer in an all-poetry bookstore in 1977. Hugh Miller, Bookseller was located on Crown Street in New Haven. There were several thousand fine press and small press books in the store and Art Beck's *The Discovery of Music* (Ellensburg, WA: Vagabond Press, 1977) was one of them. The book contains one of my favorite poems, entitled "Fog." I quote the poem in full:

> My first hundred years of death I'd
> like to spend driving down this
> same road through the hills, the
> same kind of music on the radio—Pergolesi,
> Vivaldi, Telemann, over and over—never wanting
> to stop, just continuing in the fog until I
> manage to forget everything.
>
> Only after that, maybe
> a town on the coast, another coast, a
> seacoast I don't know, just a spot of
> sun between the cliffs, and a village,
> three or four bars, some houses, a hotel. A place
> with umbrellas outside for lunch . . . That's
> strange. The bartender. With the cigaret
> in his mouth, absently washing the glasses. I think
> he was my friend, my sworn ally when I was ten.
> He has that same belonging look. And the waiter.
> Leaning against the tree. Isn't he—the old man—

Chepok! My Grandfather's drinking buddy.
And there at the corner table,
relaxing, reading her book, waiting for someone. Is
this where she lives now? My love on
the first day I met her.

It is not only an arrestingly seductive poem in depicting beauty in its own particularity, which by doing so summons Jack Gilbert's exemplary poetry, but also marks Art Beck's own astonishment with perpetuity—in this case with the peculiarities of the afterlife. However, to focus on one of Beck's main themes, perpetuity, as both homage and as a mirror for contemporary society itself, we, as readers would need to be aware of his own creative and publishing history to fully appreciate how fine an American poet and translator this man truly is.

The Insistent Island is Beck's second chapbook from Magra Books, with his first being *Epigrams: Marcus Valerius Martialis* (Translated with an afterthought by Art Beck). Beck's erudition might be the initial characteristic which any reader would take notice, and this might just earn him designation as a poet's poet; but this is a designation that is apt.

To see that there is a connection, through Beck's concern with perpetuity, from *The Discovery of Music* to *The Insistent Island* is quite clear. Beck's vision is largely classical, and to envision truth metaphorically, as well as, perhaps, metaphysically, on a seacoast or an island, for him, is as natural as revisiting the California coast or Homer's Troy, as well as Greece itself in Rainer Maria Rilke's poem, "Archaic Torso of Apollo."

Beck's love and passion for the chapbook is also clear since he has published several fine collections—each not only themed but also scrupulously selected works of poetry, all of which can be described in one word, impeccable, in the quality of the writing itself. Some of these titles include *Enlightenment: Notes for a Scurrilous Life—The Rediscovered Poems of Giacomo Casaova* (Fairfax and Los Angeles: Red Hill Press, 1977) and *Summer with All Its Clothes Off* (Westbury, NY: Gravida, 2005).

However, an avid reader of Art Beck might instantly notice that *The Insistent Island* establishes this work as not only masterful but also in etching a perennial philosophy similarly as Rodin chiseled his last masterpieces in Meudon. The blurb for *The Insistent Island* on the Magra Books website reads that it "is a hybrid work, neither essay nor translation, but a poetic response to the myriad incarnations of the Odyssey; particularly Samuel Butler's prose translation as lodged in Beck's memory via a 1980s audio book rendition. The poems were written over some thirty years, finding their synergy unplanned and unexpected. Like Homer's originals, best taken with food and drink and, of course, a pinch of salt. Drawings by Michele Lombardelli."

Beck himself states significantly, "I don't know how conscious of this I was when writing the sequence. But what strikes me now, especially after reading Madeline Miller's wonderful Circe, is that at the heart of the Odyssey is Odysseus' great refusal' to accept the gift of divinity from Calypso. A theme, with variations, that seems to run through many of the classical Greek masterpieces. Achilles choice of an early glorious death over peaceful long life. On the opposite side of that coin, the tragedy that came from Oedipus' parents refusing to accept their fate. And Oedipus' final, sacramental acceptance that, in effect, 'mortal' is a synonym for 'human.'"

The chapbook contains twelve poems that constitute a "Homage to Ithaca." Beck's voice is familiar to his readers in the opening poem of the sequence, "Penelope," where she is "Flirting with one, then another, feeling/ this one's tattooed muscles, dropping a dirty/ remark to the blond with the razor spear." Such familiarity is Beck's brand of social criticism, the bite of sarcasm in the face of reality, a dose of dark humor as anodyne, a palliative, or counterpoint, which zeroes in where there is a paucity of anyone who abandons their moral compass.

In "Telemachus" Beck first posits "So when Athena flittered down/ and became an old man, it was no surprise.// They listened." But then admonishes, " . . . Get out while you can . . . / Don't ever come back here/ without your father."

Perhaps the most accomplished shorter poem of the sequence is "The Sirens." Beck is often at his best when his target is darkness itself. This is not to indicate that his poems are sullen or bleak, nor does he lower the bar of his poetic art by falling to sheer descriptive verse, but it is through his achievement of lyric poetry, one with a message for all humanity, in which his work shines.

> What surprised him — so helpless and expectant —
> was that the sound was something else than sound.
> A sense of sunlight in the ear, a fragrance
> that could only be heard and then a wing
> and the utter joy of flight. As much beyond music
> as harmony transcends speech. A heartleap
> into a resonance so god-like he suddenly
> knew what it was the gods worshipped.
> And all this from the tonsils of three
> wretched crones who sang as mindlessly as
> spiders weave. Hunger is treacherous.

In "Being a Poet," Beck provides yet another offering of a poetic gem, and his language is not so strikingly similar in its characterization of Homer, yet with both the elegance of and reminiscent of the poetry of James Wright in how the blind Greek narrative poet "might somehow avoid his own/ dark trip into those ant caves where/ millions upon millions patiently work." However, it is in how Beck concludes the poem that he makes it memorable, "Countless, breathless eyes/ caught up in our every word." If that is Beck's take on the art of poetry, then it is an extraordinary, as well as an accurate, image that he has crafted.

Any review of *The Insistent Island* would be remiss without at least a mention of "Kalypso," with Hermes and Circe providing challenge to Ulysses, who "staggered out of the pounding/ surf: parched, speechless, and blind with/ salt, trembling, like a soon to be sacrificed/ lamb." For Ulysses it would be a period in which "Circe had him for a year" (with Kalypso), one in which he "lost track of time," and through his experiences with her, he finally "asked if he might be allowed to go/ home to die with his old wife, after which she thinks, 'I've had the best of him. The rest/ is nothing but loss.'"

Philosophizing isn't normally aesthetically prudent in most poetry, especially since most writers aren't poets enough to write well enough to portray it appropriately, but Art Beck accomplishes that in the sequence's concluding poem, "Pork." Many poets might have tried to write that "who" but the "swineherd Eumaeus" could "in the end" be the one who "saves their bacon/ at the slaughter of the gluttonous," but this is one poet who sure can. Beck closes the poem, and the sequence, with a perennial philosophy worth noting:

And your chest swells while you smile
never suspecting you're just a blur
in nearsighted old Homer's
book-ruined eyes. That it's the platter
in your greasy fingers he's trying
to tempt within reach.

An aspect of harmony and balance not to be missed in the construction of *The Insistent Island* is that Beck closes the selection of poems with two sonnets, a poetic form of which he is a master; so that there are fourteen poems in the volume, as there are fourteen lines in a sonnet. This lends a further dimensionality to the chapbook, and, thus, instills a sturdy classicism and elegance within the work itself.

One of the more insightful, and gifted, translators of Rilke, Beck includes a translation of the German poet's "Archaic Torso of Apollo." Since there are so many translations of this poem how could Beck possibly translate it differently enough to make it unique? Well, Beck has; and this translation of what may be Rilke's most famous poem belongs next to those of other translations that are also remarkable as those of Stephen Mitchell's and Edward Snow's. This work by Beck alone is worth the price of this book. In fact, it would be unfair to quote it in full in a review, however, it is nearly impossible not to include a portion of it, so that readers will order a copy of this volume for this alone, as in these last concluding verses of the poem:

> If not, this would only be a fragment
> of mutilated stone under the shoulders' transparent
> slump. Wouldn't glisten, anymore than a predator's
>
> fur, or leap like radiating star fire.
> Because there isn't any single part of t that isn't
> watching you. You have to live another life.

This translation is so fine because, like Beck's other translations of Rilke, especially his Orpheus sonnets, the language sizzles like a live wire through the poem — in harmony with both Rilke's tone and imagery, with his meaning and his vision — truly, like no one else's but possibly the original itself.

Readers should take note that the last poem in the book, "Archaic Torso," is in keeping with elements of the Odyssey itself. This is especially so in that it is like life itself. Similarly, as Lorine Niedecker, the Wisconsin native who was considered a 20th-century Emily Dickinson, inferred that writing poetry was, indeed, like "weeping a deep trickle," making using her hand pump as metaphor. "That Day at the Met" written while on vacation in New York City, is noted to have been written between the years 1999 and 2018. It is a remarkable and memorable poem for any number of reasons, but it is itself a kind of artifact. It even begins, singing about its perpetuity, quietly, like a voice heard from the past: "what really whispered to me were not/ the remnants of their useless gods." It ends more like the final cadences of a symphony — one in which we find ourselves grateful not only to have heard but to find solace, and blessing n our first having ears and the sense of hearing itself to be able to listen to:

> . . . Abandoned lines from decades ago in an almost
> discarded vacation notebook. So many since lost,
> unforeseen, gone. So many new reasons to again be so
> haunted by the breath in those dead stones.

Magra Books takes its name from the eponymous region in the Lunigiana region of Tuscany, a watershed that rises above the Appenine and flows southwest into the celebrated Gulf of Poets, which is demarcated between Lerici and La Spezia. This is appropriate for the instance of Art Beck's work, since it reflects the classicism of the work itself.

The Magra Books website states that the press is located "somewhere between Echo Park (Los Angeles) and Bagnone (Provincia di Massa-Carrara, Italy)." At least for the work of Art Beck, it is apt for Magra Books to publish "works that feature unique works by important writers," since his poetry deservedly belongs to literature of global significance, since it resonates from a dais that is not only international, but also worldly, due to its tenor and substance.

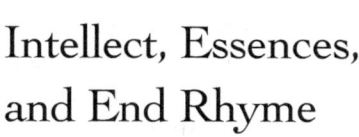

Intellect, Essences, and End Rhyme

James B. Nicola's *Wind in the Cave* and *Natural Tendencies*

THE TITLE OF JAMES B. NICOLA'S RECENT collection of eighty-eight poems references a phrase from the eminent American lyrical poet, Theodore Roethke, "My desire's a wind trapped in a cave." How eponymously apt it is, since it mirrors the poems that Nicola offers us—as scrolls unwound in the air. "Night Writer," the opening poem, is reminiscent of Constantine Cavafy, when Nicola writes "There is/ a distinguishing feature to every love . . . it's time to die again, and write."

Nicola is a poet of essences, and a master of end rhyme. A nature poem of some achievement but also an accomplished Ghazal, "A Single Rose," exemplifies Nicola's proficient sense of craft, "And baby's breath, too, and a cooling fern, and wrap them in dull paper, like a passion./ (I'll give a single rose, but it might burn.)"

However, it is Nicola's incisive intelligence that readers will be rewarded with, time and again, as in the opening of "Torn," when he writes: "If, in a *billet-doux*, you made a blunder/ but caught the gaffe in time, you could reject/ it, once upon a time, sliding it under/ your blotter to revise."

Yet it is the poignance Nicola evinces, in "veil," that the natural world and human emotion are wedded in the piquancy of image that he truly excels, "Feeling every breeze/ on your moistened face—Being:/ stung by sweet thorns," which also reminds us, again, of Cavafy, both in emotive element but also in aesthetic value.

This is a book of poetic heft, a much larger book than is usually published by Finishing Line Press, of Georgetown, Kentucky, in 2017, that is perhaps best exhibited in the poem "Weight," when Nicola writes, expansively, even hauntingly, and with such an adept touch: "the weight of me, my body, brought/ to light by the desire/ to reach the higher, brighter place/ just within my sight;/ to freely bask, and breathe, and walk,/ and ease the heft, with light." Writing such as this is reminiscent of Walt Whitman, and resonates in what are, indeed, some of this poet's better lines.

In James B. Nicola's *Natural Tendencies*, published by Cervena Barva Press, out of Somerville, Massachusetts, we "can still taste the wild and green aroma" of his landscapes — both of the interior and the natural world.

His robust imaginative intelligence is on display in poems such as "After the ice storm," where he can't keep from hearing the branches of the willows tinkling in the yards "cogitating/ and coming up like invisible confetti."

In "The Succulent," Nicola adeptly uses rhyme to portray a prickly vegetation in a barren landscape: "To what secret it owes/ its leathern flower/ and lasting power,/ no one really knows." The poem "Each tree is a now," one of the more ontological poems in the collection, exhibits true depth in the lines: "the tree stands upright/ like you and me/ deepest parts hidden in a cold, moist dark."

Nicola's intellect is prone to keep itself honed in these poems, as in the Lorine Niedeckeresque poem, "sansevierra's," whose entirety is compressed into three crystalline lines: "sansevierra's/ blade accreting crustiness/ tended, keeps quiet." And in "The Case of Stars," reminiscent of Theodore Roethke, Nicola's touch is lyrical and his tone is adept, in some of the finest lines in the collection, "The stars don't only twinkle, writhe/ and wink, but with our mindless, blithe/ emergencies, will breathe, as if, alive."

Moreover, as in the poem, "Thoreau," these poems address "This wonderment,/ This universe" in an age when green space is vanishing and the climate is warming. In response to this, although Nicola intimates "The Center may not Hold," there is a solace and a resonance to be found in the poems found in *Natural Tendencies* — demonstrated in their adept craft and uniquely adroit voice.

Art Beck's Translation of M. Valerius Martialis's *Mea Roma: The Poetic Practice of Erudition, Sophistication, and Urbanity*

Martial: Mea Roma: A Meditative Sampling from M. Valerius Martialis by Art Beck, Bristol, U.K.: Shearsman Books, 2018

AMONG MY MANY FAVORITE BOOKS OF POETRY in translation, including W. S. Merwin's translation of Pablo Neruda's *Twenty Love Poems and a Song of Despair*, Robert Bly's translation of the "first modern Norwegian poet," Rolf Jacobsen's *The Roads Have Come to an End Now*, and Edmund Keeley's and Philip Sherrard's translation of C. P. Cavafy's *Collected Poems*, there is a new addition: Art Beck's translation of the Roman poet Martial (40–104 CE) in a unique and refreshing selection just published by Shearsman Books, in England. Beck's selection of Martial is entitled *Marital: Mea Roma: A Meditative Sampling from M. Valerius Martialis*.

Beck has already been honored with an award for his translations of Martial in the 2018 American Literary Translators Association (ALTA) Cliff Becker Prize. The citation for Beck's work reads: "Art Beck allows Martial to speak directly to the modern reader, artfully navigating the profound differences between contemporary English poetry and Latin poetry of the First Century C.E. Like Martial's originals, Beck's translations are funny, beautifully crafted, and, often, profoundly shocking to modern sensibilities." Beck's Martial is, indeed, shocking to "modern sensibilities," due to Martial's compulsion to depict the blood sports of the Roman Colosseum in such gut-wrenchingly clear imagery.

So, why do we read Martial? Beck's answer in his introduction is insightful and worldly: "We never ask why we enjoy reading and watching dramatizations . . . of the early Roman Empire . . . even when he [Martial] makes us cringe. We enjoy him in large part because he speaks so directly to us; timelessly honest as it were . . . " The treat— or "illusion if you will—of being taken for a stroll around streets and posh villas of Martial's 'mea Roma.' [It is] a pleasure akin to historical fiction, or more properly, the historical resonance of a unique, primary source voice." What further separates Beck's Martial from many other translators and translations is both his erudition and his sensibilities as a poet himself. Poems such as Beck's masterful "Fog," from an early book of his, entitled *The Discovery of Music*, establish him as a major American voice, if not a "poet's poet." His erudition is on display in "Mea Roma" from his comparing Loeb Classic editions to quoting Harvard Classicist Kathleen Coleman. In the contemporary era of Trumpian corruption it seems to be perfect timing for this new translation of Beck's Martial to be made available.

Certainly it is a time when we apparently lack sensibility and erudition, or discernment, of any kind on both the Democratic left, what is often directionless and lacks a backbone, and the ultra-conservative right, which lacks moral judgment of any kind and by omission gives approbation to gross corruptions by the Trump administration. What more of a perfect time to pick up Art Beck's insightful translation of M. Valerius Martialis and to read Sp. 11, from *Liber Spectaculorum*:

> The rhinoceros pacing, Caesar, circling the arena,
> delivered even more of a fight than promised!
> Ah, how it lowered that terrible horn and charged in such a rage.
> One hell of a bull, who tossed that bull like a rag doll!

These "spectacles" are not the ones we see daily, in our era, but what we do observe is that certain human compunctions have not altered much in some two thousand years. We, too, all well know the pain of being in submission to a hierarchal amoral government under the rule of Trumpian chaos, as in these lines from "Sp. 18:"

> The marvel of the bull snatched up from the middle of the arena
> into the firmament, wasn't the stagecraft, but its submission.

Or, as in these lines from "Sp. 36":

To submit to power and to survive is also to win.
But the consolation prize weighs heavily on the heart.

However, there is also the pure aesthetic and philosophic truth that Beck not so much captures but so perspicaciously exhibits, as in Book VIII of *Liber Spectaculorum*, 51.

Asper's picked a flawless beauty, but Asper's blind. Proof again,
from a man in love: Beauty's so much more than meets the eye.

And the contemporary era of Trumpian megalomania, excess, and corruption seems reflected in the chaos of the colosseum in Art Beck's new presentation of imperial Rome: to be perfect timing for this new presentation of Martial's Imperial Rome to arrive. What better time to pick up Beck's insightful translation and read:

You dump your belly's burden, Bassus, in a grimacing gold
    chamber pot.
And toast yourself with a water glass, while your money goes to shit.

Or in these vignettes from the gore of the Roman Arena:

The way a seething bull, prodded around the arena by burning
goads, tosses one taunting rag dummy after another to the stars.
How it's finished off by fervid tusks; finally enraged enough to imagine
an elephant might be tossed as easily.

That same elephant, who just now was so brutal to
a bull, piously kneels and reveres you, Caesar.
Believe me, no trainer coached or commanded this.
He just senses the presence of our god.

Beck's Martial is cerebral, sophisticated, and urbane. As we grapple with our own age of unreason and moral collapse, Beck's Martial provides an uneasy mirror, and in so doing forces us to conclude and to re-conclude where we have been, as a human race, and where can we possibly be going. However, in the interim, we, as readers, do get a moment to ponder our current circumstances, as Martial observes:

The privileged, Auctus, rage and prosper.
Hate costs nothing, benevolence is expensive.

Novel as Painting

The Tiger's Wife by Tea Obreht

LEAD SENTENCES OF MONUMENTAL NOVELS can be memorable. Gabriel García Márquez opens his *One Hundred Years of Solitude* with Colonel Aurelio Buendia facing a firing squad and thinking about his grandfather telling him the story about the time he had "discovered ice." Francine Prose opens her inimitable American classic, *Household Saints*, with how a bride was won in a game of pinochle, "It happened by the grace of God that Joseph Santangelo won his wife in a card game." Tea Obreht opens her novel, *The Tiger's Wife*, in an impressionistic prose style, which is kept buoyant throughout the entire novel: "In my earliest memory, my grandfather is bald as a stone and he takes me to see the tigers. He puts on his hat, his big-buttoned raincoat, and I wear my lacquered shoes and red velvet dress."

Obreht is, indeed, a painter and her palette includes not only the entire alphabet of words but their own hue of colors. *The Tiger's Wife* is a postmodern folktale with all of the rich embellishments that one might expect from both the folk tradition and a sense of a rupture of postmodern society. Natalia, the novel's main character, is on a mission of mercy at an orphanage beside the sea in a Balkan country attempting to heal deep rifts after years of armed conflict. While Natalia and her lifelong friend, Zora, finish inoculating the children there, she begins to perceive the secrets pervading the very landscape around her. She also experiences a deep and haunting mystery surrounding her grandfather's death, which she attempts to plumb.

Questions abound within her: why did her grandfather, a renowned physician, choose to die in a tumbledown outpost which no one in her family had ever heard of before? Why did he exile himself? These are some of the reasons why Natalia begins her hero's journey.

Afflicted with heartache, Natalia attempts to explore what her grandfather's state of mind may have been that precipitated his departure. She plumbs the recollection of their weekly trips to the zoo when he would read to her from a well-worn copy of Rudyard Kipling's *The Jungle Book*. He also told stories of his encounters over many years with "the deathless man," an extraordinary immortal and a vagabond who apparently never aged. She also recollects her grandfather telling her the tale of a snowbound winter during World War II when the Nazis were kept at bay due to impassable roads deep in snow. Natalia never forgot her grandfather's descriptions of the frightening presence of a tiger: hunting, on the prowl, lurking in the wintry darkness.

When an unwitting blacksmith kills himself accidentally, the tiger is opportunistic, but ever mysterious. Obreht writes, ". . . he was ready to fire, strangely calm with the tiger there, almost on him, its whiskers so close and surprisingly bright and rigid. At last, it was done, and he tossed the ramrod aside and peered into the barrel, just to be sure, and blew his own head off with a thunderclap." What shivers we may feel from reading Obreht's prose prove to be as icy as they are memorable.

Although essentially being a tale regarding a deaf-mute girl who befriends an escaped tiger who fled the zoo, when Obreht was asked to summarize *The Tiger's Wife* by a journalist at Cornell University, her *alma mater*, she replied, "It's a family saga that takes place in a fictionalized province of the Balkans. It's about a female narrator and her relationship to her grandfather, who's a doctor. It's a saga about doctors and their relationships to death throughout all these wars in the Balkans."

Writing in *The New York Review of Books*, Pulitzer Prize-winning poet Charles Simic wrote that "Tea Obreht is an extraordinarily talented writer, skilled at combining different types of narrative—from objective depiction of events to stories mixing the fabulous and the real—in a way that brings to mind the novels of Mikhail Bulgakov, Gabriel García Márquez, and Milorad Pavić, the Serbian author of *Dictionary of the Khazars*." Other reviewers cited Obreht's ability to blend "fact and folklore, ritual and superstition" together with "astonishing immediacy and presence." At twenty-five, Obreht was feted as the youngest recipient of the prestigious Orange Prize for Fiction, in 2011, which recognizes "excellence, originality and accessibility in women's writing from throughout the world." The prize then included an amount of £30,000 cash and the "Bessie," a limited edition bronze figurine. *The Tiger's Wife* was also cited as a finalist for the National Book Award for Fiction.

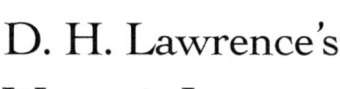

D. H. Lawrence's
Women in Love

Seeking What Is beyond the Realm of What Is Human and What Is Humanly Divine

D. H. LAWRENCE ADDRESSES LOVE IN MANY of its permutations in this iconoclastic novel of ecstasy and tragedy. The four main characters in the novel both soar and struggle in their relationships with each other and seek higher resolve in a myriad of ways despite their failures in achieving the relationship they seek.

The Brangwen sisters, Ursula, the older, and Gudrun, the younger, are emblematic of early twentieth-century women in search of love and freedom, not particularly in any specific order. They are hardly time-bound in the Edwardian era, as the novel takes place circa the early teens, since contemporary twenty-first-century women also struggle and yield to the same issues which are framed within a more modern context.

Lawrence interjects one counterpoint after another in *Women in Love*. It is a novel of many contrasting pairs of relationships, all running parallel to each other in that they are dysfunctional, on some level, but never quite the same ones. Whereas Ursula and Rupert are more psycho-spiritual mates, Gudrun and Gerald are more drawn to the raw sexual energies in each other. With that said, Ursula proclaims herself as a woman who wants to feel the sand between her toes, who needs to be sexually satisfied, but one who also responds to Rupert's more ephemeral predilections.

In contrast to these two main couples, Lawrence also interjects the counterpoint of Ursula and

Gudrun's parents who struggle after years of marriage. However, it is this couple, of the long-married variety, who are able to dodge and weave enough in their own separate lives to save their relationship, which they both deeply value, as much as it is often intolerable. In this, *Women in Love* is a novel of one dynamic juxtaposed against another: Gerald's high station in society versus Gudrun's archetype of a pure aesthetic, Ursula's earthy sexuality versus Rupert's intellectualizing and nearly quixotic search for ideals.

Seeking resolve in the modern age is an essential journey for the characters in this novel. They not so much search for relief of their burdens and the choices they have made but they look to possibly integrate the results of their life decisions. Lawrence's portrayal of these struggles evoke the painful interaction between the sexes in the modernist period and beyond, in a timeless relevance in our own contemporary society.

Gerald represents the prototypical male archetype. He needs to fix what is broken. His strength and capabilities are formidable, even heroic. Rupert, on the other hand, seeks a tautology for his philosophical and spiritual dialectic. He seeks what is possibly beyond the realm of what is human and what is humanly divine.

Gerald Crich, the wealthy industrialist, and Rupert Birkin, the ideologue, become the lovers of Gudrun and Ursula, respectively. Gerald is haunted by the deaths in his family, including his accidentally killing his brother as a boy; the tragic drowning of his beautiful sister, Diana Crich, at a water party; and his father's culmination after a long sickness.

Ursula meets Rupert after a brutal love affair with a British soldier of Polish heritage, Anton Skrebensky, as depicted in this novel's prequel, *The Rainbow*. She is attracted to Rupert in opposition to the animal passions of Skrebensky.

Gerald pays Gudrun a visit after his father's death by covertly entering the Brangwen family home where he and Gudrun make love is revelatory and bold, at once. It is somewhat shocking—by its not transcending boundaries but by vaulting over them, even in the world of today. However much Gerald is comforted by Gudrun, and as much as their relationship escalates and deepens, there is also the intimation that Gerald's embattled psyche and resilient masculinity may not survive Gudrun's innate love and need of freedom.

When Loerke, a diminutive, but brash, artist from Germany, enters Gudrun's life, as the two couples travel to the Tyrolean Alps, Gerald's rage only encourages Gudrun's attraction to Loerke. This psychological vortex engulfs both Gudrun and Gerald: as he rages she only rejects him more. Gudrun's bitterness emerges in wounding Gerald verbally, which leads to his attempt to strangle her. In relinquishing his hold on Gudrun's throat, the two are irrevocably separated: Gudrun in self-righteousness, Gerald in his abject aloneness.

In response to the loss of Gudrun, Gerald takes to the pathless snowy mountains, where he is found frozen to death. Ursula and Rupert, who had left earlier to try to give Gudrun and Gerald space to work out their relationship, are called back by Gudrun, who is coldly contemptuous in light of what Gerald chose to do.

Gudrun decides to travel to Germany after Gerald's death to continue on with her Bohemian lifestyle, pursuing an ethos of unbound freedom and pure aesthetic. Earlier in the novel, there is a wrestling scene in which Gerald and Rupert are portrayed in a homoerotic fashion. Ursula would like to be everything to Rupert; whereas, Rupert resists in reciprocating to Ursula in this way because he holds Gerald's friendship with equal respect and reverence as his love for her.

Following the saga of three generations in *The Rainbow* from the post-industrialized age to the industrial era, the main characters in *Women in Love* are loosely based on personages Lawrence knew well, especially in his portrayal of Rupert, as himself, as a man in search of ideals but one who was also physically weakened, as he was, by various maladies.

The fact that Lawrence himself was conflicted sheds much light on the characters in *Women in Love*. He was an early proponent of women's liberation and sexual freedom; however, in nearly complete opposition to this he was politically far right of center. Described as not quite being a fascist but believing in the value of an authoritarian over a social construct, for instance, put him in the direct line of fire with the philosopher Bertrand Russell, whose far left of center ideologies fueled his intellect and his passions.

Similarly, as with Lawrence's own conflicted character, the response to *Women in Love* has been historically a forceful one: either laudatory or vilified. Martin Secker, Lawrence's London publisher initially backed out off publishing the novel in 1920. Thomas Seltzer, an American publisher, first published the novel in a limited edition of 1,250 copies. It was not until 1921 did the novel find publication in a trade edition in England. This began a civil suit brought on by Lady Ottoline Morrell who claimed her likeness was too obvious as the character Hermione Roddice in the novel.

However, that is mild in comparison to reviewers who criticized *Women in Love* for its steamy eroticism. One early reviewer referred to the book as "dirt." Later critical appraisals included renown authors such as Simone de Beauvoir, who found, despite the novel's liberal and progressive treatment of women, *Women in Love* to be "chauvinistic" and overly focused on the psychologically and physical aspect of the male phallus.

Although, surprisingly, contemporary feminist and critic, Camille Paglia, has praised *Women in Love* in the early influence it had on her own literary coming of age. She even has compared the significance of the work to Edmund Spenser's *The Fairie Queen*, first published in 1590. Paglia's support of the novel is in her approbation of male sexual relations.

Late eminent literary critic and scholar, Harold Bloom, mainstay on the faculty at Yale University, considered *Women in Love* to be among the most influential novels in the canon of Western literature.

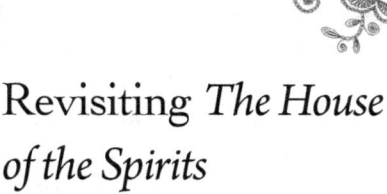

Revisiting *The House of the Spirits*

Mysticism, Love, and Magical Surrealism

ALTHOUGH THERE ARE SEVERAL COMPETITIVE themes vying for the one central theme in *The House of the Spirits*, atonement, both divine and secular, runs deeply through Isabel Allende's debut novel. Coming to atone for various shortcomings in vision and compassion as well as outright crimes perpetrated by one of the novel's main characters, Esteban Trueba, perpetuate through a multi-generational absolution. What is crucial for resolve here is the attending consciousness of making atonement, which is intrinsic to its achievement, either full or partial—which also includes the significant act of forgiveness itself.

There is a strong current of feminism throughout the novel. Specifically, it can be referred to as a feminist view of history or even a proactive feminist historical perspective. The main female characters in the novel—Clara, Blanca, and Alba—who represent three generations of the del Valle-Trueba clan, are the purveyors of the true, and vast, family history. Political strongmen are seen as deleting truth or creating fake news for the sake of their regime, but it is women who are able to tell the tale truthfully. Ultimately, this also provides the opportunities for both atonement, then forgiveness, which is fluidly woven into the central theme.

The level of mysticism infused in *The House of the Spirits* is thoroughly enchanting. Clara often practices psychokinesis. She is also a clairvoyant, and predicts her sister's death. The death of her sister—mermaid-like, with green hair—Rosa the Beautiful, although an early tragedy, also reveals the vulnerability in those psychically empowered. Through this Allende imparts that some of us may be able to move tables and predict the future, but we are all not immune from various tragic life experiences, such as the death of a loved one.

There is a dynamic of politics that is at the core of *The House of the Spirits*. When Esteban Trueba, then a hard leaning conservative, supports a junta against the government, he lacks the clarity of vision to see that it can, as it does, go far astray, and that the military dictatorship which he has helped install in his country proves to be unsafe for everyone. Ostensibly, Allende portrays the Pinochet coup d'état in Chile, in 1972, which she uses as an historical reference and which the novel shadows. In doing so, there is a struggle between socialism and fascism, and it is in the end which socialism triumphs.

It is the element of love which is the existential glue that holds *The House of the Spirits* together, ultimately. It is the spark of love between Esteban Trueba and Clara Del Valle, at the beginning that sets them ablaze with love. It is the love Esteban has for his granddaughter, Alba (meaning "dawn," in Spanish), which is persevering in that it leads to the possibility of Esteban's eventual atonement, and what provides the dynamism for Alba's magnanimous forgiveness of what has happened in the past for the del Valle-Trueba family. Essentially, also, it is Alba's love for her grandfather that provides her the strength and the hope to break the karmic chain of revenge and hatred exhibited through the improvident practice of patriarchy.

As Allende's character, Alba, says in *The House of the Spirits*, "the space of a single life is brief, passing so quickly that we never get a chance to see the relationship between events; we cannot gauge the consequences of our acts, and we believe in the fiction of the past, present, and the future, but it may also be true that everything happens simultaneously." There are some physicists who believe that this is in fact possible and correct—that everything is, indeed, occurring at once. In light of this, Allende has not only written a brilliant family saga worthy of lengthy feminist critique, which also addresses the hostility of fascism, but has created a metaphysical fiction for the ages. She even prefaces the novel with a quote from Nobel Laureate, Chilean poet Pablo Neruda: "How much does a man live, after all?/ Does he live a thousand days, or one only?/ For a week, or for several centuries?/ How long does a man spend dying?/ What does it mean to say 'for ever'?"

The Neruda quote only presages a novel that begins and ends with the same phrase: "Barabbas came to us by sea . . ." The child Clara writes that in her journal at the book's beginning and Alba reads her grandmother's words in that same journal decades later, "written in a child's delicate calligraphy," as the novel's last words. In this, Allende creates a mythos in the book, alpha beginning it and alpha ending it, a dialectic resolved, an entire mythology, a feminist generational history, complete unto itself. It is stratagem and diadem, alike. It is multi-generational but dissolving into the timelessness it arose from and arising from the timelessness of our lives: alchemy and magic, at once.

What is significant is the portrayal of the severe male character of Esteban Truebo, the often cruel patron of Las Tres Marias, the family hacienda; the sometimes overbearing husband of Clara, and the harsh father of Blanca, whom he alienates when he cuts off three fingers of one of the hands of socialist revolutionary Pedro Tercero Garcia (whom is said to be modeled after folksinger Victor Jara) because Blanca and he were lovers.

Although feminist criticism rightfully condemns Esteban for his many wrongs, such as raping peasant women, such as Pancha Garcia, who births his bastard son, Esteban Garcia, Esteban's character exhibits a transcendence from his incontrovertible and unyielding maleness, even a *machismo*, to transcend his previous actions, at least partially, through his acknowledgment of his crimes and misdemeanors, thereby atoning for them, especially in his helping Blanca and Pedro Tercero escape the junta to flee to Canada; then later in his petitioning his old friend, the prostitute, Transito Soto, who had influence with the military, in releasing his granddaughter Alba from her being held in a concentration camp.

Although his wife, Clara, kept her promise to never speak to him again after he knocked several of her teeth out in an argument relating to Blanca and Pedro having become lovers, on his deathbed, with his granddaughter Alba by his side, Esteban's conscience is ameliorated in knowing that Clara has forgiven him, from beyond the grave, as he dies peacefully. It is then that Blanca begins to read her grandmother's notebooks, "Barabbas came to us by the sea . . ."

Written in a style known as Magical Surrealism, Isabel Allende creates a family saga not dissimilar to Gabriel Garcia Marquez's *One Hundred Years of Solitude*, published some twelve years earlier. Magical Surrealism employs paranormal events, mysticism, mythology, alchemy, and magic in establishing a mystic realm which appears to be more real than life itself. Through this literary necromancy, Allende, as does Marquez, creates a timeless world where past affects present, which then portends the future.

The House of the Spirits, although a work of Magical Surrealism, is also considered partially autobiographical and certainly historical, especially the parts of the novel regarding the coup d'état, since the author is the niece of Salvador Allende, president of Chile from 1970–1973, was overthrown by CIA-backed fascist strongman Augusto Pinochet, whose military arrested, tortured, and assassinated many Chileans, including many artists and writers, such as folksinger and guitarist, Victor Jara, whose hands and fingers were broken by Pinochet's soldiers, but who continued to sing an anthem of freedom to his fellow countrymen in the soccer stadium they were imprisoned in, until he was shot multiple times. His body was said to have been shot by some forty bullets.

Sometime before her composing *The House of the Spirits*, Allende translated several romance novels into Spanish, most notably the work of renowned romance writer Barbara Cartland. Allende attributes her inspiration to writing *The House of the Spirits* to a long telephone conversation she had with her then ninety-nine-year-old grandfather, who was near death at the time. She began writing the novel after her composing a letter to her grandfather, which became the basis for the novel itself. Since she started writing the book on January 8, every novel she has begun after that she also beings on the same date.

Initially, *The House of the Spirits* was rejected by several notable South American publishing houses before being published in Buenos Aires, in 1982. Upon publication, the novel nearly instantaneously made Isabel Allende an international literary success. She was awarded not only with the Best Novel of the Year in Chile but since then the book has also been translated in more than thirty-seven different languages worldwide.

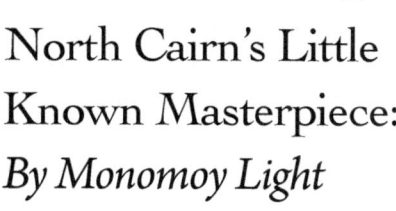

North Cairn's Little Known Masterpiece:
By Monomoy Light

Nature and Healing in an Island Sanctuary

NORTH CAIRN'S *BY MONOMOY LIGHT:
Nature and Healing in an Island Sanctuary* is a modern
classic of nonfiction writing. Books by authors that
come to mind whose prose invites comparison include
Peter Matthiessen's *The Snow Leopard* and John
McPhee's *Coming into the Country*.

However, actually, Cairn's book *By Monomoy
Light* is an underappreciated and little known gem.
The nature writing in the book is nonpareil. Also, the
courage in the portrayal of Cairn's healing due to
childhood abuse by a father is enormously heroic and
moving. Harper Lee's *To Kill a Mockingbird* made her
famous throughout her long life. Lee wrote just one
book, and who could possibly say that she could top
that masterpiece.

Cairn's masterpiece is relatively unknown. She,
too, has written one accomplished work, but this one
is nonfiction and not fiction. Cairn may eschew fame,
and that is evident in the rigorously integral prose she
carves elegantly and powerfully in the language of
her personal narrative and her tale of the Monomoy
Islands. The reader intuits her solitude and the solace
she find in it.

If any reader is seeking a rare find, an impeccable
work of prose, a heroic journey, and a transcendental
ascendancy, North Cairn's *By Monomoy Light* will
provide all of that and more. Her book is filled with
the mystery of the land and of the mystical lure of the
sea. Her prose stings with salt. Her story is as endlessly

lyrical as the waves of the ocean are in relation to the rhythms of her sentences.

Cairn's American masterpiece is ruminative and rhapsodic at once. It is a book, not unlike Harper Lee's, in which the author has created a work so nearly perfect that she possibly didn't need to write another word; and in this we can actually listen to the intermittent hush of the sea in the space between the words in her story.

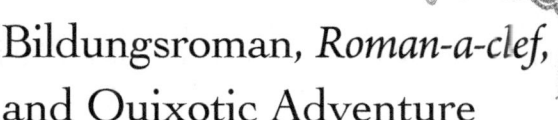

Bildungsroman, *Roman-a-clef*, and Quixotic Adventure

Hans Christian Andersen's
The Improvisatore, *A New Translation,*
by Frank Hugus

IN 1976, I VIVIDLY RECALL CARRYING AROUND Mark Strand's and Charles Simic's *Another Republic*. It was the first anthology, in my estimation, to be published that largely contained European and South American authors whose work infrequently, if not rarely, was translated into English. I remember reading Carlos Drummond de Andrade, Zbigniew Herbert, Czeslaw Milosz, and Francis Ponge for the first time.

As a reader and a bookseller coming of age in the Yale community, I privately dubbed the contemporary era that of the golden age of translation. However, I had already read Gregory Rabassa's translations of Gabriel Garcia-Marquez, Ralph Mannheim's translations of Hermann Hesse, and Robert Bly's translations of Knut Hamsun.

I had nearly memorized W. S. Merwin's eminent translation of Pablo Neruda's *Twenty Love Poems and a Song of Despair*, which was published in 1969, and since then has not been surpassed. Frank Hugus carries on this modern tradition of translation in his bringing Hans Christian Andersen's *The Improvisatore* freshly into existence. Nearly a century before E. M. Forrester and D. H. Lawrence fell in love with Italy for the entire English-speaking world to come to know, Andersen did so in Danish for the Danes.

The Improvisatore is a kind of Bildungsroman, a *roman-a-clef*, part Quixotic adventure part travelogue, semi-autobiographical social romance, not without a somewhat precocious pro-feminist commentary. The novel, historically, easily rests beside Goethe's *The Sorrows of Young Werther* and the best of Dickens, of which I would cite my own favorite, *Bleak House*, for its alacrity and for providing a further definition to what the novel, as a literary vehicle, could become, could achieve, and, of course, could inspire.

Although there have been other translations of Andersen and at least one other translation of *The Improvisatore*, this version by Frank Hugus renders the best intent of Andersen's Danish. The work is crafted by Hugus to take into account what the most accurate English translation from the Danish means while being in harmony with how the English translation reads. To strike this balance is what the accomplishment of an imminent translator is, from any one language to another, and Frank Hugus's translation of *The Improvisatore* is nothing less than an achievement.

Although this novel does not appear on either *The New Yorker* or *The New York Times's* summer reading lists, it should. The novel should not only be brought to the beach to be enjoyed as a sophisticated read, it is also a perfect book to look toward for course adoptions for both literature and language courses. The subtitle of this work, *A Novel of Italy*, says it all, and no one but Hans Christian Andersen, in Frank Hugus's new translation, says it any better.

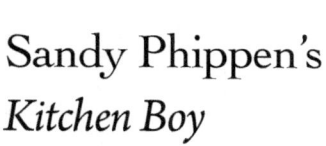

Sandy Phippen's
Kitchen Boy

The Classic Great American Novel

IT IS NECESSARY TO PLACE *KITCHEN BOY* BY
Sandy Phippen into its proper context. Phippen has
written a classic great American novel that can be
placed next to books such as *Town and the City* by
Jack Kerouac and *Been Down So Long It Looks Like
Up to Me* by Richard Farina.

If readers initially respond to the historical context
that this places *Kitchen Boy* in, and that being the
late 1940s to the mid-1960s, then that response is an
appropriate one. Phippen replicates the period between
1958 and 1965 with such accuracy in his prose that the
tastes and smells from the "Kennedy era" come alive
off each and every page of this fine book.

An example being Chapter 41, in which Phippen
writes with memorable alacrity the August morning
of 1962 when news of Marilyn Monroe's death filled
the consciousness of Americans that sunny summer
morning. This particular chapter is also significant for
Phippen's portrayal of Mia, one of the coworkers of
the book's protagonist, Andy Harrison, the "kitchen
boy" of the summer Manor. The older woman, Mia,
instructs the young man, Andy, how to dance, and in
doing so, the writing reveals a stunning intimacy: not
one illustrating sexuality, per se, but the alchemy of
eros, including the ever-so-delicate inflection of the
dynamic of feminine psychology and the portrayal of
its power and not its "machisma."

Kitchen Boy is an American classic that Grace
Metalious's "Peyton Place" is not. Not unlike one of
Andy Harrison's favorite author's, Thomas Wolfe, the
prose of this book evokes a distinct and clarion image

of the times which surround the coming of age of American youth during this era. Also, unlike many books written by a male writer, especially during this period and later, *Kitchen Boy* is peopled with female characters: both those growing into adulthood and those in charge of their own lives as well as in counseling and informing the lives of others. Phippen is perhaps one of the most celebratory of writers concerning the feminine psyche. Although in keeping to the accuracy of his vision, the writing in *Kitchen Boy* does not circumnavigate the dark side of either the era or his characters.

Sandy Phippen has written an American classic. If "beach reading" is what any reader is seeking, then *Kitchen Boy* certainly fills that requirement, especially in the book's honest portrayal of "summer people" and the "Maniacs" who are their servants; however, it is also an addition to the canon of American literature, and the book can be placed among the very best writers of the twentieth and twenty-first centuries.

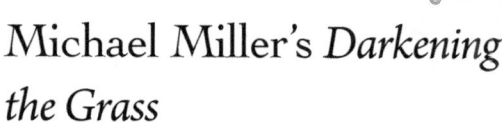

Michael Miller's *Darkening the Grass*

The Transcendence of Death

THE TWENTIETH-CENTURY GERMAN POET Rainer Maria Rilke suggested that the responsibility of critics was to reinterpret literary works every generation and the task of poets and writers to create new works for posterity. In an age of literary solipsism in the early twenty-first century, critics, in a fashion similar to politicians who perpetrate often misinformed arguments to disavow their opponents, often appear to sharply gouge open especially significant contributions of poetry by authors in an attempt of bolstering themselves above their intended victims, as if pathetically employing a mode of Darwinian evolution of the survival of the fittest to suit their own perpetuity. What occurs in this maddening literary politic is that often enough there are books of poetry of true value to the genre itself, and even of a caliber of a greater literary and humanistic resonance, that are lost amid the mediocrity of what is published and much of what is called poetry in America.

Darkening the Grass is the poet Michael Miller's third full-length book of poetry. In a conversation I once had with the Israeli poet Yehuda Amichai, Amichai posited you could refer to yourself as being a poet only if you were in the act of writing poetry. However, the poems of Michael Miller are always writing themselves with each reading and perpetually working in the mind, much of the time, with the music of the songs that they are.

Darkening the Grass was selected for *Emerging Voices* of CavanKerry Press. His previous volumes include *The Joyful Dark*, the Editor's Choice winner of the McGovern Prize at Ashland University Press and the beautiful letterpress limited edition published by Birch Brook Press, *The Singing Inside*. He also has published several books with Pinyon Publishing since the original writing of this essay.

The thirty-three poems in *Darkening the Grass* are distinguished by their polished poetic line; the sense of each being a separate work of achievement within themselves, and contributing to the theme of each of the book's six sections, or movements; and then each section becoming a part of its symphonic whole. This book offers itself as a perfect definition of what a synecdoche is: a part that is reflective of the whole, or a whole reflecting each part. Miller's poem "Cutting An Orange," quoted in part below, is emblematic of an attribute such as this.

> Each morning I cut an orange into halves
> And the halves into quarters, trying to make
> Each segment equal, cutting evenly, precisely,
> Beginning the day with this small claim
> To order. You turn from a dream
> At the noise I make in the kitchen.
> Valencia, Seville, I whisper,
> As though we were making love,
> Then place the wedges on a plate.

If Miller were a composer of music he would be more of a Brahms than a Mozart, more of a Samuel Barber than an Aaron Copeland. His poetic predecessors include the too often overlooked American imagist poet, Bert Meyers, especially in that both are also their own masters of the poetic sequence; the lyric poet Samuel Menashe, a recent winner of the Neglected Masters Award from the Poetry Foundation; and Donald Justice for the control and the precision of his language, as well as his sensitivity to both the classic and the humane.

Unlike many books of poetry, in which there may be a number of passable poems in various sections of each collection, each section of *Darkening the Grass* contains only a few offerings, with the qualitative difference that every poem in each of this book's sections are memorable. In the first section alone, each poem could easily be a nominee for any respectable anthology, perhaps most especially the one from which the source of this book's title is derived, "On The Sunlit Field." Few poems have the capacity to either be referred to as a nature poem or a political poem worth being dedicated to memory. Even fewer poems are said to be both. Almost none at all can profess to possibly bring readers from the far right or the far left together, in a kind of healing, over what is the travesty of senseless tragedy.

Like a sail in the windswept air
The one raised wing
Caught our eyes as we walked
Upon the sunlit field
And saw this bird,
A headless eagle
With that one raised wing,
A gravestone now,
Beside the bullet shells
Darkening the grass.

"Each Day," a sequence of thirteen poem that comprises the second section of this book, addresses one of Miller's major themes, aging and death. However, it is Miller's own perennial philosophy of living each day and every day to its fullest that, mot unlike Robert Frost, becomes one of his own "momentary stays against confusion." In the Joycean stream of the unconscious emanating through "Each Day," Miller enables the reader to discover in the persona of "Bill" a celebration of the epiphany in the commonplace, that extended and beautifully protracted sense of eternity in an action that only lasts perhaps just a moment.

VIII
When they arrive at the feeder
Fluttering in the still air,
He tries to sing as beautifully
As he can to the cedar waxwings
With silvery gray feathers
And yellow-tipped tails.
They pay no attention
To the songs which draw him
Out of his shrunken body
And allow him to feel,
Momentarily, so happy.

When we may next make a list of our poets who have written memorably of war — such as Michael Casey, in his Yale Younger Poet Award-winning book, *Obscenities*; or Brian Turner, in his Beatrice Hawley Award-winning collection, *Here, Bullet* — may we be sure to include the war poems and poetic tributes to soldiers by Michael Miller. The third section of *Darkening the Grass* offers poems of a similarly distinct gritty voice and a full-throated tenor.

"Young Marines" depicts a friendship of what the term *Semper*

Fidelis means to a young marine who is haunted in his recollection of "My friend" who "advanced ahead of me/ On a jungle trail where leaves hid/ Trip-wires, spider webs for the wary." The poem ends in gut-wrenching eulogy.

> An instant later I picked limbs
> Out of the trees and placed them in
> A body bag that I am still carrying.

"Listening At The VFW" is a poem that is exemplary of Miller's ability for poetic etching and lasting achievement in depicting an insightful character portrait; whereas other poets may have only been able to provide a simple sketch. The elderly veteran at the VFW he observes has "stripped his words to truth;" and "rolls up his sleeves/ Challenges a man/ Half his age to arm wrestle;" where "Between shots of bourbon/ At the corner table" he positions "His back" that is "always to the wall;" and who in "His eighty-fifth year/ With a lifted glass" the poet has the humility in being "Afraid to tell him/ Anything, knowing/ He has heard it all."

Miller ratchets up the level of poignance among these poems regarding soldiers and war in the pieces to which he directly affixes a fictional name as poem title: "Private First Class Lawler," who "was sent to Ramadi/ From Wilmington, Vermont,/ And here a sniper/ Is looking for him;" or "Sergeant Reese" who dreams of "Fly-fishing at sunrise, the Swift River/ A blue road bending between towers/ Of pine and hemlock and his yellow line/ Whistling through the peaceful air;" and Lieutenant Dempsey," who, suffering from PTSD, needs to remind himself that the call of a "blue jay/ Perched on a one branch" is not "an incoming mortar/ Before it explodes." However, it is in portraying a lover's hand tenderly touching the amputation of a returning soldier that Miller makes his case against war despite his loyalty and fealty to each soldier and every marine.

> Her hand strokes
> His stump
> Which feels like
> The smooth top of
> The Louisville Slugger
> He swung as a boy
> On the hot fields of
> Greenville, Tennessee

In section four of *Darkening the Grass*, Miller not only returns to his leitmotif of death but also to how we may deal proactively with the all too finite aspects of our lives. The poem "Moving" is layered in one image after another of transition, and moves with a verbal agility from one image to the next. "Books stacked in boxes" are "like his body/ Packed in its coffin." The poem ends in his needing to "keep the illusion/ That if he never moved/ He wouldn't be an inch closer/ To the next landlord, death." It is a kind of inverse poetical statement in comparison to Mark Strand's famous poem, "Keeping Things Whole," in which Strand has his metaphysical "reasons for moving;" however both poems parallel each other in qualitative accomplishment.

"The Wolf," a poem in eight parts, is a sequence that easily could be placed next to Prokofiev's symphonic orchestration, *Peter and the Wolf*, and perhaps the former may even be more haunting as a poem for adults than the latter is a fairy tale for children. The "wolf" Miller portrays is a metaphor for death. Throughout the poem he throws off fear of the wolf like he would a worn woolen blanket when he rises to begin his day. It is a poem of heroic proportion that suggests a Sisyphean struggle with death itself, as in the poem's concluding section.

VIII
He walks beneath trees.
Their leaves tilting with light.
Wherever the wolf has gone,
Outcast, cut off
From all things human,
It waits for the dark to return.

The entirety of section five of *Darkening the Grass* is the eighty-two line poem, "The Alien Begins His Day," a work that was initially published in *Ontario Review*, and that establishes Miller's range in that he is also quite capable of crafting a longer narrative poem as well as s shorter lyric. It is a fictional meditation of a man recounting his life — "in the continual journey which turns in his mind/ Like the cards in an old woman's hand." The poem resolves itself in the affirmative, in which he trusts what "will bring him closer to love,/ To all that appears alien, like the bones/ In the earth like the fugitive notes/ Of the full-hearted bird beginning to sing."

The last section of this accomplished collection of poetry concludes with poems that offer a kind of *coloratura*, a distinguished virtuoso exhibition of Miller's lyricism at the apex of his craft. There are definite anthology pieces collected here: "meadowlarks and sonnets/ Sing inside his head" in "Mowing;" in "Flight" he imagines his wife's and his "aging" body to be "pressed close, like feathers;" "Marriage"

is an ode to what may still be honored by both word and the act of
husbandry when he attends to his wife who "shivers" and "He warms
her with each/ Essential part of him;" and in "The Flowers" when he
may be too old or too ill he imagines he will still see "her garden/ A
dazzle of flowers brightening/ Their front yard, the lilies/ Like trumpets
pointing toward the sun,/ The irises like twists of sea and sky."

However, "Wildwood Cemetery" maybe the only one of what
may be considered among Michael Miller's candidates for a signature
poem; for it, truly intimates, not unlike what Walt Whitman discovers
in section fifty-two of "Song of Myself," or what Mary Oliver achieves
in "White Owl Flies Into and Out of the Field," the transcendence of
death in vigorously living life itself.

Each dawn he walks where sleepers never waken
And when he sees a fox like a streak of flame
Flashing across the grass oblivious to
The gravestones or a file of turkeys strutting
Through a doorway of leaves or a raccoon
Waddling like an old man with heavy pockets,
The dread of death he carries like a tarnished coin
Vanishes as a goldfinch rises toward the sky.

Anonymous Gifts

In the Spirit of Alan Swallow's
Short Story "Golden Girl"

NEARLY TEN WINTERS AGO, I RECEIVED A letter from my employers on Christmas Eve that I would no longer be needed at my job, after having announced that they were looking forward to seeing me back in the office after a two-week holiday break, not uncustomary in the publishing business. What I remember is the sharp pain, after having read the letter, which cut through me as I walked back from the mailbox on the road, envelope in hand. With the amount of the enclosed paycheck from the last two weeks I had worked, along with the bonuses I had earned, I would be able to cover the costs of rent and bills for the month, then into the middle of January, however no farther than that. The holiday season, itself, acted as a kind of panacea. Although I practiced the art of frugality often enough, since I was devoted to being a working writer, who was either often enough unemployed, and between either freelancing assignments, or underemployed, and between jobs outside of my writing studio that often enough provided me with the grist of a post-doctoral course on the practice of humility, as well as a catch-as-catch-can existence. I made a point of waking up every morning in gratitude that I had two good feet to place on the wide-planked yellow pine floor and two fine arms to raise to the ceiling in praise of the grace of just being alive and well, in honor of the simple pleasures of being able to enjoy my meals and my friends.

However in the evanescence of the passing of the holiday season, by mid-January, I felt the walls closing in regarding to even my careful allotment of funds to cover expenses. Even with my normal amount of fervent optimism, few employers were interested in hiring a white male who was nearly sixty. Not only the weight of financial responsibilities pressed itself upon me, with a stress that actually felt as if I were being crushed beneath it, but also a career of almost forty years that was passionately spent in pursuing books and publishing, on all levels and in every way, all seemed for naught. The result of this was my fear of losing my living space, which I loved, in a refurbished farm house located amid preserved farm land, but also for my becoming homeless in, of all seasons, winter in New England, where January can be harsh, but February characteristically guaranteeing a monthlong deep freeze and at least one batten-down-the-hatches Nor'easter. So, I paid a visit to the person closest to me in the entire world, my lover who evolved into something indefinably beyond that—someone whom I shared in being a spiritual steward for each other, someone in whom I did not have a conventional relationship with but with whom I experienced, and delighted in, a mutually and psychically intimate lasting bond.

Although I often scrupulously listened to her voice her own concerns and questions, regarding the practice and the path, and the mystical and the practical, when I visited her one January Monday afternoon, she knew something was amiss with me. After I informed her of my having lost my job, as well as when and how, the light in her face changed intensity, and I witnessed the determination infuse her visage. Within the weeks that followed, and which my friend informed me would occur, she phoned everyone she was aware of who knew me in conjunction with the local library, and queried them as to whether they would send me an anonymous donation through the mail to assist me in weathering at least the winter, to help me to keep the fierce winter wolf from my door until I could possibly find work in the spring, to be able to keep warm within the solitude of my home.

For days on end and for several weeks from early February onward to mid-April, anonymous cards and letters, without return addresses, arrived, in ones and twos, and sometimes even in threes, in my mailbox, bearing amounts of one or two twenty dollar bills, or an unaddressed check for twenty-five or fifty dollars, with which I paid my rent and covered my expenses. This was the miracle of an extraordinary friendship and the miracle of the mailbox, whose karma reversed itself in having initially born the news of a lost job into provisions of many gifts of sustenance and support.

Der Blaue Reiter Group

Steven Schroeder, David Breeden, and *Daodejing*

IF A SIMILAR DER BLAUE REITER GROUP OF pre-World War I artists were present today, that included the likes of Wassily Kandinsky and Arnold Schoenberg, Steven Schroeder might be the artist Franz Marc, a leading member of the group, who is known for his iconic and mythological painting titled "Blue Horse."

Steve is a keen editor, a renowned publisher, and an accomplished poet. However, neither does the list of his accomplishments stop there, they only begin to broaden. To my knowledge, as a colleague and friend, the breadth of Steve's work is what could only be described as that rarity, I believe, especially in the early twenty-first century where specialization is the norm—a modern Renaissance man.

For instance, and most recently, I know of a gorgeous sequence of poems he has written regarding modern mystic Dietrich Bonhoeffer; a powerful poem regarding the painting of Paul Klee; a significant essay he crafted with respect to Hegelian philosophy in conjunction to the poetry of John Donne; and if you visit his website, you may find a painting of a cactus blossom rendered in oils on the right hand page that, for me, offers that perennial mystique of the divine found in the art of Odilon Redon. Steve's painting entitled "Cholla Blossom 2," in my opinion, also perpetuates an incandescent realm of the sacred.

Steve perhaps may be better described as a painter, a poet, and writer who has spent some years moonlighting as a philosophy professor teaching at the University of Chicago's Graham School—largely in an interdisciplinary setting. He earned a Ph.D. in Ethics and Society from the University of Chicago and a B.A. in Psychology at Valparaiso University. He also claims that since he grew up in the Texas Panhandle, that emptiness plays a large role in his painting and poetry.

He writes that he usually focuses on a single image and that his paintings often contain what isn't there as much as what is. Although he also writes that his hope is that his work invites more than it contains.

It is an enduring honor for Steve to invite me to participate in what became a rigorously interactive interpretation of *Daodejing*, along with poet and writer, David Breeden. For me that is and will always be a once in a lifetime opportunity to be a part of a project which resulted in three poets creating three parallel renderings of the work of whom Steve has referred so appropriately to as "our old master." All three of us had been reading various translations of Lao Tzu for more than forty years.

With Steve exercising such beneficent invitations to David and myself, what occurred can be said to be a kind of perfect storm of literary congeniality and felicity that precipitated a creative synergy which was like none other I have experienced in my writing life. What resulted through Steve's vision of bringing us together is a unique, and I believe relevant, new version of the intended words of "our old master."

My process in what I term rendering Laozi was initially reading the translation that Steve Schroeder would present in the Google Docs program, which I would then copy into my hardcover journal whose sole purpose was a workbook for *Daodejing*. My approach was to place myself in the forefront of Steve's translation with an amount of veneration, then, and this was always crucial, to find, and more appropriately discover, where the lyric core of the poem arose from. When I found that, then my own rendering flowed. However, it may have been one or two of the middle lines, perhaps an image at the end, and most usually, especially toward the conclusion of *Daodejing*, with the beginning lines, that I was able to locate the source of the flow of each particular verse.

My attempt was not only to render "our old teacher," Laozi, but to also play off of Steve's translation—much like how John Coltrane released the sweet torrent of sound from his saxophone in harmonizing with Johnny Hartman's voice, and Johnny Hartman's debonair baritone rising to meet that effusion of Coltrane's grace notes—but also my purpose was to limn Steve's meaning; to shadow a phrase, here and there; and to offer both clarity and a mirror to the perpetuity of the Laozi's import and wisdom.

I first came across the Gia-Fu Feng and Jane English translation of Laozi when I was twenty, over forty years ago in New Haven, when I was also reading every Eastern classic I could assimilate, as well as practicing Zazen with a small group of people in the basement of Yale Divinity School Chapel. Although I augmented my reading of Steve's translations with the Fu and English version, and often enough chose to strike a balance between the two to actually and effectively fashion a new rendering, I have also treasured Ursula K. LeGuin's translation, as well as Stephen Mitchell's, who, on occasion, as I recall, was one of the other participants in sitting meditation in the basement at the Divinity School Chapel, when he was grad student at Yale.

My being invited to render Laozi has been completing an enormous circle for me, as Joseph Campbell, whose voluminous works of comparative religion and mythology I have studied, might point out as being the hero's journey. In that time it is not only Campbell who I found both inspiration and guidance from, much after my discovery of Laozi, but also the psycho-spirituality of the modern mystic Carolyn Myss, and the high octane spirituality of *The Guide Lectures*, channeled by Eva Pierrakos, among many others, whose writing regarding higher consciousness have affected me, such as Pema Chodron, Katherine MacCoun, and Eckhart Tolle—all of whose insights, at least partially, I have integrated, and that have lent themselves to becoming some of the very philosophical underpinnings of my renderings of *Daodejing*.

It is with gratitude, and an active humility, that I thank everyone here that I have mentioned by name, including, of course, 'our old master,' as well as for Yinxi, the sentry at the western gate, who, apocryphally or not, stopped Laozi, and asked him to record his wisdom before moving on, into the frontier, beyond, which as a result was *Daodejing*—for it is as if I have come to meet them both, stepping out of the western frontier of the future, to greet them in the eternal now, in which we all have come together, with our hands placed firmly palm to palm, bowing to one another, in unison.

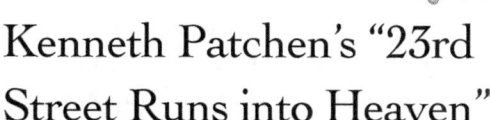

Kenneth Patchen's "23rd Street Runs into Heaven"

Extolling an Immemorial Poem

I FIRST READ KENNETH PATCHEN'S "23RD Street Runs in to Heaven" when I was in my late teens while collecting all of the Pocket Poets editions published by City Lights. *The Love Poems of Kenneth Patchen* stood out for me because of "23rd Street Runs into Heaven." I still think of it as a perfect poem, although at the time I first read it never would I have thought of it as an immemorial poem. What it means to me now, a half century later, and how I read the poem is completely different than how I first read the poem. The difference is that I initially read the poem in a romantic light, with desire and passion flickering within the margins; whereas, now I read the poem as a testament to active loving on a mature and deeply moving humane level.

"23rd Street Runs into Heaven" is just more than a poet's poem and much more than just a favorite poem. When you live with a poem for several decades you realize why poetry meant something to you in the first place. Some of the other poems that fit that category for me are Art Beck's "Fog," James Wright's "A Blessing," Seamus Heaney's "Oysters," and Jack Gilbert's "A Brief for the Defense," in no particular order. These poems are much like an opera lover's favorite arias. They are talismans. They are healing prayers. They are the best of old friends.

There are not many people that I have known that are aware of "23rd Street Runs into Heaven." In 2012, when I was invited to be the opening reader in the Devil's Kitchen literary festival held at Southern Illinois University in Carbondale, due to my having been the cowinner of the Crab Orchard Series in Poetry Open Competition, one of my colleagues at the weeklong event, who was also invited to attend, just happened to mention "23rd Street Runs into Heaven" in a lecture he was giving. For a prose writer, and not a poet, to have cited the Patchen poem with such respect brought an uncharacteristic nonverbal utterance from within me, issuing out of my mouth, which had dropped open in sheer surprise. Trying to cover for myself, since I am normally not known for such a loud outburst that made others in the seats in front of me turn to look at who could have made such a noise, I leaned toward the cohost of the event and tried to portray what had arose from such depths within me was due to the poem mentioned being one of nearly unutterable beauty and uniquely significant in its deftness of craft. Instead, my embarrassment faded somewhat into a deep appreciation of the poem being cited in the first place and that perhaps my nonverbal burst of delight might have led others to not only reference the poem, and read it, but to also sip the poem's contents like one does with a cherished crystal glass containing the G. E. Massenez Crème de Cassis de Lyon that one savors before dinner.

Judging by the copyrights listed for *The Love Poems of Kenneth Patchen*, in the edition I own, the poems were composed between 1939 and 1965, the latter year being the publication date of the book. However, I believe we can discern that the poem was written in the 1940s or 1950s due to the "newsboys" starting "their murder-into-pennies round." Somehow, I have always imagined the *noir* that Patchen creates to be similar to that of a film starring Humphrey Bogart, such as *The Maltese Falcon*, which was filmed in San Francisco, and the "before-supper Sabbath" being an innocent one—with, albeit, an unforeseen and possibly marauding darkness lurking in the shadows. Here is the first verse of the poem:

> You stand near the window as lights wink
> On along the street. Somewhere a trolley, taking
> Shopgirls and clerks home, clatters through
> This before-supper Sabbath. An alley cat cries
> To find the garbage cans sealed; newsboys
> Begin their murder-into pennies round.

This can be considered the first verse of a sonnet—a mid-twentieth-century American sonnet. The lines are taught and they conjure a tone of warmth and a certain timbre: the background noise of a city on an early Saturday night. This first verse delineates the framework for elemental human comfort, a pause in the work week, a sense of one's being on the very cusp of experiencing some rest, if not repose.

The next eight lines finish the sonnet and explicate why "23rd Street Runs into Heaven" is such an accomplished poem. At first, decades ago, I was infused with the poem's indelible portrayal of two lovers settling in together for a night at home, the intimacy that Patchen creates with just a few masterful images, the sacredness of that intimacy, and the honoring of how much humans, everywhere, yearn for that to have happened at least once in their lives, to have been able to store that immemorial, priceless evening in their memory for all time. These lines are not only cinematic, they are also lyrically melodious. They form both film and soundtrack. Their visceral romantic sweep are nothing less than extraordinary—but what we also find in the every day and nearly ordinary. It is what I term finding the numinous in the commonplace.

We are shut in, secure for a little, safe until
Tomorrow. You slip your dress off, roll down
Your stockings, careful against runs. Naked now,
With soft light on soft flesh, you pause
For a moment; turn and face me —
Smile in a way that only women know
Who have lain long with their lover
And are made more virginal.

The poem could have concluded there. The last line of the verse, "And are made more virginal" astounds one with its gravity. The sense of awe that is infused in the reader leaves one in a state of gratitude that resembles a cloud of bliss which can last for a small forever. We are not only left with a sense of profundity but a real feeling of what it truly means to be alive—something few poems offer. However, let's hold that feeling for just a moment and let us focus now on the poem's final line, which after a half a century of rereading it I have finally come to the conclusion that Patchen may have added the line to the finished sonnet as an afterthought, that the poem had been written, perhaps on a sheet of paper, and he added the line afterward, after the initial heat of composition. And this is how he finished it: "Our supper is plain but we are very wonderful."

This line cinches it. We have gone from the profound to the ordinary and in this juxtaposition we enter the realm of the extraordinary, the transcendent, the immemorial. This poem presents us with this gift. Actually, this poem itself is a gift. How absolutely human we not only feel but also how consummately human we actually have become.

Rich or poor, isn't this what we want and need to experience in our relatively brief lives? Isn't this what the Buddha had in mind when after finishing a lecture he looked into the throng of listeners in front of him and he saw his disciple Kashyapa hold up a flower, upon which the Buddha transmitted direct *prajna* (wisdom) as Kashyapa bowed his head in understanding. As Joseph Campbell relayed, "Life has no meaning, life is an experience." Kenneth Patchen gives his readers such an experience in "23rd Street Runs into Heaven."

However, what I've learned these last fifty years is that although the last line of "23rd Street Runs into Heaven" does propel the poem into a kind of radiance, what I didn't at all understand was how a woman could be "made more virginal." The poem, I had thought, was a testament to what is sensual, to the celebration of lovers, to the sanctity of intimacy itself. Also, I had thought early on, in what was sheer poetic reverie, that Patchen was describing the indescribable: a woman who has "lain long with their lover/ And are made more virginal."

What I've come to understand, only recently, is that none of that is true, or at least not all of it is. What I've come to comprehend, especially after my own experience with my partner, Tevis, is that women are, indeed, "more virginal," in actuality, if they have "lain long with their lover," since the scene that Patchen describes is rather quite ordinary. It is so ordinary that the two lovers have transcended the sensual, and possibly the sexual, and that they have become so at one with each other that common sensuality is certainly a touchstone to their sanctity of intimacy. But it is in what is truly sacred we find in the commonness of "soft light on soft flesh" so much so that their awareness of the oneness of each other is not dependent at all upon it. They have gone beyond it. Their oneness is such that their "supper is plain" although "they are very wonderful." They have experienced their communion plainly and have been transubstantiated by it.

"23rd Street Runs into Heaven" is as much a poem of transcendence as it is of love, as much about love as it regards the transubstantiation of the flesh, as much as physical alchemy as the sacramental act of "our supper" being "plain but we are very wonderful." It is as much as Kashyapa holding up the flower in acknowledgment of having understood the Buddha's sermon as it is about Joseph Campbell guiding us into the wisdom of our not wanting an explanation of the mystery of life as much as actually experiencing it fully.

"23rd Street Runs into Heaven" is all of those things, and more, just like every immemorial poem is—and after a lifetime of reading and recommending poems there sometimes seems to be so very few of the quality and resonance of this poem. This Kenneth Patchen poem is one I have absolutely loved extolling, and passing it on to you, so that you can then extol it to others. In this, I believe lies both the mystery of life and the experience of living it, which is what the best poetry can, and does, perpetuate in what is immemorial about it.

PART III

Selected Reviews

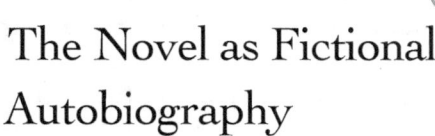

The Novel as Fictional Autobiography

Loitering with Intent by Muriel Spark

IN MURIEL SPARK'S SIXTEENTH NOVEL, *Loitering with Intent*, she has created a dynamic character, Fleur Talbot, who seems to be reminiscent of Spark herself as young writer. Fleur, in this fictional biography of a novelist, looks back upon the nascence of her first novel and the unusual incidents surrounding the launching of her successful literary career. At the onset of the book she is jobless, and known as a writer only on the periphery of London's literary scene. But Fleur rejoices in several things: that she is living in the twentieth century, that she is a woman, and that she "loiters with intent," seeing people as they actually are.

In spite of having published only a few poems in some little magazines, she has begun her first novel, *Warrender Chase*. To support herself while writing it, she must find work. A friend recommends her for a secretarial position with Sir Quentin Oliver, the founder of a little-known organization, the Autobiographical Association, who is also a snob. Fleur is hired, and for the next ten months of her life — September 1949 to June 1950 — she finds herself involved in a series of bizarre and somewhat comical events.

Sir Quentin informs Fleur that he created the Autobiographical Association so that the life stories of a handful of people of his own choosing, whose histories might otherwise have gone overlooked, should be preserved in writing. His plan, after the stories of their lives are finished, is to lock them away in a vault for seventy years, when these autobiographies will be released for public perusal. Fleur's job is to edit these writings and rewrite them when grammar, spelling, or syntax is askew. She is quite bored by this task because she is consumed with writing her own novel. As she soon discovers, each autobiography, even in the first chapter, is a presentation of dry and uninteresting prose by and about an authentically uninteresting person.

Fleur's relationship with Sir Quentin is tentative at best, as it is with his housemaid, Beryl Tims, whom Fleur refers to as an "English Rose," a woman who is shallow, pseudo-matriarchal, and prone to religious hypocrisy. But Fleur strikes up a close friendship with Sir Quentin's mother, Lady Edwina, who, although quite aged, has a keen mind and a sharp wit. Both Sir Quentin and Beryl believe that she is hopelessly senile and try to keep her in check, but are rarely successful. Lady Edwina will often enter unannounced to the closed-door sessions of the association, pointing an accusing finger at her son and saying he thinks she is "ga-ga." She waltzes about the room in her long gown and strings of necklaces, her overly made-up face wearing a wrinkled smile, and has a "fluxive precipitation," or, simply, wets the floor. In response, Sir Quentin can only summon Beryl to usher his mother out of the room, whimpering, "Mummy!" This greatly amuses Fleur, for her work for the association is generally devoid of excitement. Also, she knows that Lady Edwina is not incontinent, but has her "fluxive precipitations" to upset Sir Quentin, Beryl, and the association.

The members of Sir Quentin's association, all either rich, titled, or ecclesiastical, are a singularly eclectic group that share one characteristic: they are weak-minded. The group includes Sir Eric Findlay, a sugar-refining merchant; Lady Bernice "Bucks" Gilbert, a widow who clings to her upper-class mannerisms although she is no longer well-to-do; Baronne Clotilde du Loiret, who espouses an established French lineage; Mrs. Wilks, whose family lived in the Czar's palace before the Russian Revolution; Miss Maisie Young, an ex-equestrienne who was crippled in a riding accident; and Father Egbert Delaney, a defrocked priest who insists he fell from grace not because of his loss of morals, but because of his loss of faith. Fleur, to Sir Quentin's glee, spices up their autobiographies to relieve her boredom in having to edit their manuscripts. For instance, during a segment in Sir Eric Findlay's tale where he remembers once being locked in a closet during the absence of his parents, she fictionalizes that his "nanny" and the butler are engaging in amorous adventures in the nursery.

Her assiduous determination to finish her novel *Warrender Chase* enables Fleur to keep going at her job. The typescript of her novel quickly accumulates to the size of the London telephone directory. In the novel, Warrender Chase, a statesman and a poet, dies in an auto crash, and his followers mourn deeply for him. Warrender's papers and letters are gathered together by Warrender's mother, Prudence, his nephew Roland, and Roland's wife, Charlotte, who plan to publish them in a book that is to be edited by an American scholar named Proudie. The investigation of his personal writings shows that Warrender, who was considered to be a moralist and always above suspicion for any misdeeds, was in fact the leader of a sadistic puritanical sect. His followers were so loyal to him that they did whatever it was that he dictated, including suicide. The public Warrender Chase, who lectured and was known to editorialize in *The New York Times* was just a mask; in reality he was a surreptitious small-time Reverend Jim Jones. What baffles Fleur in writing her novel, however, is that the characters in her book and the members of the Autobiographical Association begin to resemble each other.

This is firmly and bitterly confirmed by Fleur's best friend, Dottie, another "English Rose." Fleur had suggested to Dottie that she join the Autobiographical Association to get her mind off of losing her husband, Leslie, who had once, briefly, been Fleur's lover, but left Dottie for a young gay poet, Gray Mauser. Although Fleur cautioned her not to take Sir Quentin and his group seriously, Dottie succumbed. As Fleur claims is necessary for young writers, but regrets in retrospect, she reads her novel to a group of friends, including Dottie, for criticism or approval. Dottie believes *Warrender Chase* to be an evil book that certainly should not be published or even read. Dottie is prejudiced, though, since Leslie is writing his own novel, entitled *Two Ways*, and despite his new relationship with his gay lover, she is typing it for him. Dottie's main objection to Fleur's novel is that Fleur is writing directly about the Autobiographical Association, a fact more evil, Dottie thinks, than the book itself.

Fleur denies Dottie's accusations. She says that she started the novel even before she was employed by Sir Quentin. After the novel is finished, her friend, newspaper reporter Solly Mendelsohn, helps her to acquire a publisher, Revisson Doe of Park and Revisson Doe. She then notices not only a deterioration in the members of the association but also that Sir Quentin is using exact lines from *Warrender Chase*. When she explodes in anger at him because of his snobbish ribbing about her literary aspirations, she tells him that she has written a novel that will soon be published and that it will be a success. Sir Quentin then responds: "Don't you think you've had delusions of grandeur?" This is what Warrender says to a Greek woman in his sect who later commits suicide. Fleur leaves in a huff and quits her job with Sir Quentin, but soon discovers that Dottie fills her place as secretary for the association, whose members are all taking large doses of Dexedrine under Sir Quentin's orders in preparation for participating in various religious rites. But Fleur does not discover that Dottie has stolen the original manuscript of *Warrender Chase* until she returns home and notices its disappearance.

Unable to sleep because of the loss of her manuscript and because of an upsetting note from Revisson Doe, informing her that *Warrender Chase* will not be published (she later learns this is the doing of Sir Quentin, who has threatened to sue for libel if it is), she goes over to Dottie's apartment. There, beneath the window, she sings "Auld Lang Syne," the song they have often used to awaken one another if they need company in the middle of the night. In her confusion, Fleur thinks she sees the head of Revisson Doe poke out of Dottie's window. She cannot believe what she sees, but later discovers that Dottie was, indeed, sleeping with Revisson Doe to ensure publication of Leslie's novel.

Fleur is enraged. Aided by Lady Edwina and Gray Mauser, she sneaks into Dottie's apartment and recovers her manuscript. Lady Edwina helps by having her "fluxive precipitations," keeping Dottie busy all day. Gray Mauser lends a hands by giving Fleur the key to Dottie's apartment that Leslie had given to him. Also, helped by Lady Edwina and Solly Mendelsohn, Fleur steals the files of the Autobiographical Association so that she can reveal Sir Quentin's chicanery. Fleur leafs though the files of each member only to find that lines directly taken from *Warrender Chase* appear in them. In fact, Sir Quentin has taken on the character of Warrender Chase, coercing Lady Bernice "Bucks" Gilbert to take her own life as the Greek woman does in Fleur's novel.

Fleur sets out to put an end to Sir Quentin's moral waywardness and his villainy by demanding that he do two things—disband the association and to see a psychiatrist. After returning home, she finds that Sir Quentin has reclaimed the files she had stolen from him and has gone to his property in Northumberland, where all of his followers are waiting for him. Before he arrives, however, he is killed in an car crash, just like Warrender Chase.

At Sir Quentin's funeral, Dottie attacks Fleur verbally, accusing her of causing Sir Quentin's death because she wrote *Warrender Chase* and knew all along what was going to occur. Fleur forgives the mindless Dottie, however, and they stay friends through the years and countless husbands that follow in Dottie's tortuous personal history. Lady Edwina burns all the files of the Autobiographical Association and lives comfortably with her keen mind and sharp wit intact until her death at the age of ninety-eight. Solly finds a publisher, Triad Press, for Fleur's *Warrender Chase*, which becomes an overwhelming critical success. In fact, all the novels Fleur subsequently writes, including several she envisioned during the bizarre events in which she became enmeshed in during her employment at the Autobiographical Association, such as her *All Soul's Day* and *The English Rose*, are published under the prestigious Triad imprint.

Loitering with Intent is a complex, poetic, and hilarious novel that has a great deal of literary flair. Muriel Spark, after so much distinguished writing, has not depleted her creative talents. Readers are fortunate that there are intelligent and caring writes such as Muriel Spark who write books as rich as *Loitering with Intent*. It is a novel of integrity that is compelling to read.

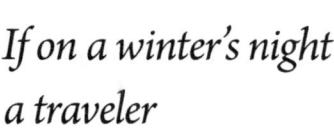

If on a winter's night a traveler

Italo Calvino's Contemporary Allegory and Literary Pyrotechnics

AS THE NARRATOR SUGGESTS IN CHAPTER ONE
of *If on a Winter's Night a Traveler*, when beginning
this book you should relax and make sure everything
you need to accompany your reading is within reach,
because concentration is the most important element.
After all, you the "Reader," have made a trip into a
bookstore and purchased the volume. There you saw
on the shelves all the books that you have been meaning
to read, that you should read, and that you would like
to read, but you avoided these temptations and chose
the newest novel by Italo Calvino, master of allegorical
fantasy. You will agree, because this book resembles a
hall of mirrors. And you, the "Reader," will become a
central character and an active participant.

Of course, you were not aware of this when you
chose the book but it contains the beginnings of ten
novels within one novel. The story begins as a man with
a mysterious cargo stops at an anonymous train station
and enters the bar. His mission is unknown to you as
his cargo. He reveals very little about himself to avoid
attracting attention and is waiting for further orders.
At the bar he strikes up a conversation with Madame
Marne, a divorcee who owns a luggage shop. Before
long, however, he receives orders to leave. An express
train grinds to a halt outside and carries him off to an
unknown destination. To your distress, just when you
are engrossed you discover a defect in the book. Pages
you have already read repeat themselves for the rest of
the book. So you make another trip to your bookseller
and find out that part of the edition has been recalled

because of the defect. Some of Calvino's novel were mixed with that of a Polish novel of Tonzio Bazakbal's, entitled *Outside the town of Malbork*. When you decide on the Bazakbal instead of the Calvino out of frustration, you then encounter the "Other Reader," who, also frustrated, has opted for the Bazakbal too. Her name is Ludmilla. Quickly, you get her phone number. Perhaps your shared passion for novels can lead to friendship.

You begin Bazakbal's novel, which is filled with characters with names such as Brigd and Gritzvi and where much of the action takes place in a kitchen that is fragrant with frying onions. But there is a defect in this book too—every other page is blank. It is impossible to follow the thread of the story. Through your own research, you discover that it is a Cimmerian, not a Polish, novel. After phoning Ludmilla, to corroborate this absurdity, you are invited to come with her to see an authority on Cimmerian literature, Professor Uzzi-Tuzii, at the university. Uzzi-Tuzii confirms the existence of such a novel in Cimmerian. Written by Ukko Ahti, the book, *Leaning from the steep slope*, deals with a sallow young man who is beguiled into helping a prisoner escape, but it, too, abruptly ends without resolution. Uzzi-Tuzii explains that this is a characteristic of Cimmerian prose. Then Ludmilla's sister, Lotaria, bursts through the door to explain that it is not the work of Cimmerian origin, but is Cimbrian and was finished under the title of *Without fear of wind or vertigo*, written under the pseudonym of Vorts Viljandi. Lotaria invites her sister and the "Reader" to attend a seminar where the novel will be discussed.

Vorts Viljandi's novel has nothing to do with Ukko Ahti's, *Without fear of wind or vertigo*, whose main characters partake in perverse sexuality, is set against a background of battling revolutionary armies. There is nothing left for you to do in this state of confusion except to go to the publishing house to see if matters can be straightened out. There you meet Mr. Cavedagna, an editor, who reveals that the translator of Viljandi's novel, Ermes Marana, did not know Cimbrian and that the novel, written by a little-known Belgian writer, Bertrand Vandervelde, was called *Looks down in the gathering shadow*. You ask if you can see the book, but Cavedagna can show you only a slim stack of photocopies. Still, you think,, this is better than nothing. In reading Vandervelde's novel, a suspense story that takes place in Paris and involves a man and a woman who are trying to get rid of the body of the man they murdered, you realize that none of these novels have anything in common with each other.

Cavedagna gives you permission to read Marana's letters, which provide a clue to the mystery of the unfinished novels. Marana is a plagiarist who is involved in both the Organization of Apocryphal

Power (OAP) and the Organization for the Electronic Production of Homogenized Literary Works (OEPHLW). The duties Marana fulfills for these organizations range from "public relations to revolutionary movements, before and after their coming to power" to testing novels on inveterate readers through the use of electronic equipment to see whether or not the novels are viable. Reading further, you find that Marana has accused Silas Flannery, a best-selling author, who currently has a writing block, of plagiarism in his latest novel, *In a network of lines that enlace*. Marana claims, word for word, it is Vandervelde's *Looks down in the gathering shadow*.

Your next discovery in your search for a complete novel is no surprise. Marana is not only guilty of plagiarism but is also culpable of calumny. *In a network of lines that enlace* is certainly not Vandervelde. It is a novel concerning a professor who is plagued by a phobia of telephones. Armed with the wealth of information you have gathered, you cannot wait to inform the "Other Reader," Ludmilla. She phones to tell you to wait for her at her apartment, and as you are perusing her books there, Irnerio, the "Nonreader," enters. Irnerio has trained himself not to read and considers books excellent material from which to construct abstract sculptures. When you discover a copy of Flannery's *In a network of lines that enlace* on her shelves you are stunned. Irnerio informs you that Marana and Ludmilla are good friends. After Irnerio's departure, Ludmilla returns home to a barrage of questions. The truth is unveiled as Ludmilla explains that Marana became a plagiarist because of his jealousy of her. Reading novels so he could become a part of every book Ludmilla read, Marana, therefore, could always command her attention.

You decide to visit Flannery yourself after coming upon *In a network of lines that intersect*, purportedly by Silas Flannery. In this novel a billionaire attempts to protect himself from kidnapping by constructing elaborate optical devices that multiply his reflection. Ludmilla decides to visit also, and Flannery appears to like the "Other Reader," but not you. Unwisely, you have told him that you intend to catch up with Marana, who is now in Japan, so Flannery writes you into a novel, entitled *On a carpet of flowers illuminated by the moon* so he can be left alone with Ludmilla. This novel, supposedly written by Takamori Ikea, portrays the erotic adventures of a Japanese student who is living in his master's household. Before you can finish it on your plane to Japan, you find yourself in Ataguitania instead, where you are jailed because the book you have with you is banned.

Before you were imprisoned, you were handed a book you believed to be by Lotaria, Ludmilla's militant sister, but this novel, also without an ending is by Calixto Bandera, entitled *Around an empty grave*. It deals with the trails of an adolescent trying to find his roots. You, the "Reader," have not had a pleasant trip to Japan, since you never arrived there, but from Ataguitania you are transferred to Ircania, where you sip tea with Arkadian Porphyrich, the Director General of the State Police Archives. Your job is to aid in the task of choosing the books to be banned. Anatoly Anatolin is working on a version of Bandera's novel, which you never had a chance to finish, in an Ircanian setting. So you attempt to get in contact with Anatolin in order to read the book. It is a novel entitled *What story down there awaits an end?* Naturally, it is nothing like Bandera's novel. The protagonist of Anatolin's possesses the gift of making things disappear. His wish is to be left alone with a young woman, Franziska, and in the process he makes the world vanish.

Despite the fact that you wind up married to Ludmillla, the "Other Reader," as in a fairy tale, at the "real" end of *If on a winter's night a traveler*, you are the "Reader," a little winded by this contemporary allegory. Calvino's literary acrobatics can be a trifle tiresome.

Calvino's novel deserves praise for its technical excellence and literary pyrotechnics. It is unique and labyrinthine. Nevertheless, some readers will not experience as much pleasure as Calvino's "Reader." Not everyone will find the conjugal bliss of marriage to Ludmilla satisfying enough, because not everyone will want to finish the book. Some readers actually may feel manipulated by the author's brilliance and will leave Calvino's traveler on a winter's night out in the cold — despite the beauty and accomplishment of the prose.

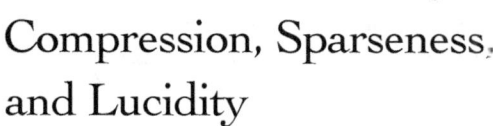

Compression, Sparseness, and Lucidity

Raymond Carver's *What We Talk about When We Talk about Love*

RAYMOND CARVER'S *WHAT WE TALK ABOUT When We Talk about Love* is a collection of modern stories about everyday people and the loss they have experienced, people that everyone knows or has known. Carver's stories are peopled with characters who feel awful, or even desperate, like the man in "Why Don't You Dance?" He assembles the furniture collected on his front lawn for a tag sale. His life obviously broken, he has lost the ability to care. When a young couple stops to see what bargains they might find, he offers them drinks, then allows them to purchase everything for next to nothing. Weeks later, they realize they have a surfeit of things they do not really want or need. They puzzle over why they bought them and why he sold them in the first place.

This kind of bizarre experience is repeated in "Viewfinder." In this sketch, a man, with chrome hooks instead of hands, knocks on the door of a suburban home. The man who answers is curious about how this person lost his hands and perversely invites him in for coffee to see how he will hold the cup. The amputee has an old Polaroid and offers to photograph the house for a small fee. Realizing that his host's family has left him, he declares that he, too, had a family once. As he holds out his chrome hooks, "They're what gave me this," he announces. His host agrees to the photo session. He wants dozens of photos. Of course, they are all photos of a man alone with an empty house.

Not all of Carver's stories have this surreal touch. "I've seen some things," says the male protagonist in "Mr.

Coffee and Mr. Fixit." What he has seen is his mother, a widow who belongs to a singles club, kissing a man on her sofa. He has seen his kids go crazy and his wife have an affair with an unemployed aerospace engineer she met at Alcoholics Anonymous. He has seen a lot, indeed, and says: "I don't know what we were thinking of in those days," in trying to explain all that happened. His wife's lover, whose name is Ross, is dubbed Mr. Fixit, by him because, ironically, Ross cannot fix anything. The protagonist imagines Mr. Fixit in the modern building where he worked with "Mr. Coffee" machines in every office. After the affair ends, he is sure the man is actually charming and intelligent because he believes his wife would otherwise not have fallen in love with him in the first place. Then he thinks of his father, who died in his sleep, drunk, and his mother, who now belongs to a singles club. When he asks his wife for an embrace before supper, all she can say is: "wash your hands." This story evokes the irrevocable iciness of events in life that can neither be changed or accepted. This is vintage Carver—a penetrating story told aesthetically but with utter simplicity.

The disintegration of marriage is one of Carver's favorite themes, and in "Gazebo," he punctuates the drama of the two characters, Duane and Holly, with dialogue in which they repeatedly use each other's name. They were teenage sweethearts who married and took on the shared job of managers of a motel. Holly did the books, Duane did the repairs. But Duane becomes involved with the Mexican chambermaid, and Holly cannot accept his unfaithfulness. she remembers how they once took a ride out into the country and stopped at a house for a glass of water. The owners, an old couple, showed them an old gazebo out back, overgrown with weeks, where musicians would play. She thought they could live out their life together like that in a dignified manner. Her dream is lost, and no matter what Duane says, it cannot change her mind.

"Sacks" is another story that touches, partly, on the same theme. A son comes to visit his father, who has recently been divorced from his wife. The son has time only for a couple of drinks at the airport bar. The father, who has bought a bag of candy and jelly beans as a gift for his daughter-in-law and grandchildren, tries to relate the painful story of his unfaithfulness, but his son lacks the concentration to listen. The father had an affair, that resulted in dissolution of his marriage, with a cosmetics saleswoman, and was caught by her truck driver husband, who cried instead of manhandling him. When his father finishes telling the story, the son leaves for his plane, forgetting the sack of sweets on the bar, too busy in a busy world, unsympathetic, cold, and unable to care. The father is hopelessly lost. This vision of parent-sibling relationships is haunting and, too many times, undeniably true.

Nor is Carver's consciousness unaffected by today's violence-prone society. In "Tell the Women We're Going" he portrays an act of senseless brutality and murder that is all too common. Bill Jamison and Jerry Roberts were friends from childhood who even purchased their first car together, a 1954 Plymouth, in their senior year of high school. They both married shortly thereafter, had jobs that were lucrative enough to give them a middle class status, and generally prospered. Every weekend Bill and his wife Linda visit Jerry's clan. Jerry has two children, and his wife Carol is pregnant again. One Sunday, the men are drinking beer while the women are doing the dishes. Jerry is restless and edgy, so he asks Bill if he wants to take "a little run" in his 1968 Chevy. Bill agrees. After a few games of billiards and a few more beers at a bar, they decide to pick up two young women they pass riding bicycles. They turn around. Bill, only literally along for the ride, is not too concerned about being able to seduce them. Jerry feels differently however, and they follow the women to a wooded area, stop the car, and then split off in two directions to try to catch them. When Bill comes upon Jerry and the women, Jerry has already picked up a rock. He uses the same rock on both women.

Another story, "The Third Thing That Killed My Father Off," reflects on the responsibilities of friendship. The narrator reveals that there were three things that contributed to his father's death: the first was Pearl Harbor, the second was moving to his grandmother's farm, and the last was Dummy. Dummy was a laborer at a sawmill in Washington. He was certainly dumb, and most people thought he was deaf too. It seemed that Dummy was quite content with his job and his wife, although she cheated on him. That was until the narrator's father showed him an ad in *Field and Stream* for a live bass that could be shipped anywhere in the United States. According to the narrator, Washington had all the trout you could fish, but no bass. Dummy bought the idea and the fish, depositing them in a large pond in the back of his property. The bass became Dummy's pride; they were the only bass in the whole state, and as far as he was concerned, it was going to stay that way. He put up an electric fence, topped by barbed wire, all around the pond. But that winter the bass in Dummy's pond were lost, and Dummy was never the same again. He went berserk, killing his wife for her infidelity, then drowning himself in his pond. The narrator's father felt responsible for Dummy's actions because he had suggested the idea of the bass in the first place. After Dummy's demise "it was so long to good times and hello to bad."

Carver deals with the inability to communicate in "A Serious Talk." Burt, divorced, can see his wife and family only on holidays. Since it is Christmas, he looks forward to seeing his children and to making amends with his wife. He arrives at his old house with an armload of gifts but is met only by punctiliousness. His wife's lover is due at six o'clock, and he is expected to leave beforehand. He dumps enough sawdust logs onto the fire to burn the house down, takes all six of the pumpkin pies his wife has baked, "one for every ten times she had ever betrayed him," and exits. Burt comes back the next day to apologize but ends up cutting the telephone cord when someone calls for his wife's lover. After the ensuing argument, he departs, resigned to having a talk with his wife after the holidays, after things have cooled down, which is what he has been trying to accomplish all along.

In the title story, "What We Talk about When We Talk about Love," two couples find themselves drinking gin and trying to spell out what love is. They are professionals approaching middle age, divorcees who have remarried. Mel leads the discussion describing his love for his wife Terri as being spiritual, and unlike the inferior love that his wife's ex-lover, Ed, had for her. When Terri left Ed, he committed suicide by shooting himself in the mouth. The other couple, who have been together for only eighteen months, Nicky and Laura, hold hands, drink, and usually say very little. By the end of the evening, however, a distance grows between them, as it does between Mel and Terri. Mel relates a story about an elderly couple that barely survived an auto wreck. They were both in casts from head to foot but the husband was depressed because he could not turn his head and see his wife who was in the bed next to him. This, alludes Mel, is love. By the time darkness falls, there is a silence between the two couples that none of them can fill.

The short stories of Raymond Carver are little masterpieces of compression, sparseness, and lucidity. His long-awaited second collection of short stories, *What We Talk about When We Talk about Love*, is marked by drama, a dynamic tension, and lyric prose.

These stories are riveting, convincing, and powerful reading, and are examinations of contemporary life that probe everyday consciousness with depth. The societal malfunctions Carver focuses on become glaringly visible. Although a cure can never be found if the symptoms are unrecognized, reading the stories in *What We Talk about When We Talk about Love* can be a healing experience if the reader is will willing to confront the ills of modern life.

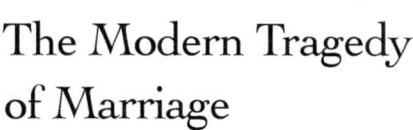

The Modern Tragedy
of Marriage

Life before Man by Margaret Atwood

MARGARET ATWOOD, IN *LIFE BEFORE MAN*, delves into the lives of three characters, Elizabeth, Nate, and Lesje, in a story of the fatigue and miseries of marriage and relationships. The story is presented in chapters entitled simply "Elizabeth." "Nate," and "Lesje," along with the date of the action. Each chapter of *Life before Man* is a first person monologue or third person narrative description of what each particular character is feeling or doing on the same day. The days are sometimes consecutive, at other times separated by weeks or months. And Atwood reaches deeply into each of their psyches to retrieve the reasons, like somber pearls, for what will bring them together and what keeps them forever separate. In the first chapter, Elizabeth is lying on her back, her clothes perfectly unwrinkled. It is as if she were laid out at a wake, and her psychological state is deathlike. Elizabeth is a woman on the edge of breakdown. She is distraught over the recent suicide of her ex-lover, Chris, who killed himself because of her, and she mourns for herself. Her husband of ten years, Nate, soon breaks an invisible thread across her doorway—one that she puts there in her mind to keep him away.

Nate has either forgotten what love is or he has never known it. He is a bumbler, apologetic from too many years spent in a broken marriage, still trying to assuage a wife he can no longer appease. Nate gave up practicing law to make wooden toys. It suits him better and is easier, although not as lucrative. They remain together because of the children, and there is an understanding between them that they may take lovers.

Elizabeth works in the city museum where she is a director of special projects. She is competent, businesslike, and urbane. Her ex-lover, Chris, worked there also. The affair was simply physical for Elizabeth, but it had a deeper meaning for Chris.

As for Lesje, who also works at the museum, her passion is dinosaur bones. Ever since she can remember, in school, she could always spell the names of dinosaurs such as Pteranodon. In her adolescent daydreams, she walks in Cretaceous swamps observing various species such as a Gorgosaurus. Lesje thinks her breasts are too small, her teeth too large, and her nose too long. She has problems in dealing with the world.

Lesje's choice of a lover reflects her shortcomings in real life. William is blonde, well-scrubbed, and from a good family. Lesje is ashamed of her family. Her grandmothers actually raised her; one was Jewish and the other Lithuanian. Although they never met, they hated each other, and, of course, never approved of their children's marriage. Lesje, angular and fragile, feels protected by William with his rich kid smile, college boy manners, and stuffy smoking room charm. For William, Lesje is non-confronting, safe, and someone whom he can intimidate whenever he likes.

Nate asks Lesje to show his children, Janet and Nancy, around the dinosaur exhibits one Saturday. She thinks this is a bit odd and believes he has ulterior motives. To Lesje, Nate seems more mature than William, and to Nate, Lesje is feminine, beautiful, and young — someone with whom he can have another chance at living his life. Lesje is tired of William's pomposity and childish antics. Nate is tired of affairs with pasty-faced secretaries from his old law firm, and of trying to pay his share of the rent by chiseling wooden giraffes. Both Lesje and Nate are tired of their lives. They have something in common, and they become lovers.

Elizabeth's reaction to Nate's new affair is vituperative and hostile. She could understand Nate's predilection for washed-up clerical workers, but she is jealous about Lesje. Lesje, the awkward and shy beauty, is a personal threat to Elizabeth, who needs Nate to keep everything running smoothly for the children. Nate's leaving her for Lesje is the cataclysmic event that could shatter her life.

The thing to do, Elizabeth decides, is to tell William what is going on. But her plan backfires. William's boyish pride is bruised by Elizabeth's eye-opening revelation, and he is hysterical. After Lesje comes home from work on the afternoon that he has learned of her unfaithfulness, he rapes her. She frees herself from him, locks herself in the bathroom, and moves out the next morning after he leaves for his job. She is determined to convince Nate to live with her, to leave Elizabeth and his children.

Nate worries over whether to leave Elizabeth and the children. Little Janet is already copying her mother's polished mannerisms, and crybaby Nancy is constantly tugging at his pants. Nate has never been very decisive, but has let the decisions make themselves. Through Lesje's obvious commitment, he feels forced to join her, yet he procrastinates about moving.

As frightening as the thought of a broken family is to Elizabeth, Nate's vacillation is too much to bear. Elizabeth grits her teeth, faces the situation, and gives Nate a push in Lesje's direction, but not without demanding child support, even though she can easily support her children.

Elizabeth's fear of the family breakup and concern for the children originates from her own tortured childhood. Her mother was an alcoholic, who died from burns received while smoking in bed obliviously drunk, and her father was a ne'er-do-well. She and her sister were raised by their aunt, a tyrannical holier-than-thou, white-gloved religious fanatic. Later, her sister had a mental breakdown and later committed suicide. This is one of the many unhealed wounds that Elizabeth bears.

The children live during the week with Elizabeth and on the weekends with Nate, who has had to resume his law practice to make ends meet. But the children's visits do not suit Lesje well. They become for her a part of Nate's former life and Elizabeth's treachery.

Lesje succumbs more and more to her regressions, considers suicide but lacks the courage to carry out her self-immolation. Nate continues to believe that she is a princess, a wonder of feminine perfection. Lesje demands more understanding from Nate than she receives. To get even, she throws away her birth control pills, deciding to have a child by Nate without his knowing and believing this might force Nate to pay the attention to her that she believes she rightfully deserves.

At the conclusion of *Life before Man*, the characters are left with their unresolved struggles. They are like three solitary dancers on three separate stages—the action stopped, the spotlight dimming. They are still mired in the subterfuge of their own lives, and they have gone in circles searching for meaning. Their lives have been altered, but everything seems to have remained the same. Like marionettes, their positions have only changed just a little bit but nothing more.

Margaret Atwood, author of several novels and books of poetry, continues to write in *Life before Man* with the same poignancy that has characterized her previous work. This is a tightly-knit story, a modern tragedy, and points to the reality that one out of every two marriages ends in divorce. Atwood presents the sorry replica of contemporary life and love with astringent clarity. She writes powerfully and with wisdom.

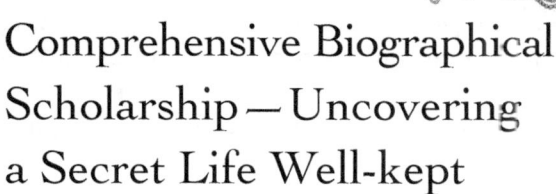

Comprehensive Biographical Scholarship — Uncovering a Secret Life Well-kept

Maughm by Ted Morgan

WILLIAM SOMERSET MAUGHM WAS BORN OF English parents on January 15, 1874, in Paris. It was the apogee of the Victorian era in England. In France, the Franco-Prussian War had recently ended with the French defeated at the hands of the Prussians. Maughm's father, Robert Ormond Maughm, had set up a partnership in law in Paris in the late 1840s. In 1863, he married Edith Mary Snell, a delicately beautiful woman seventeen years his junior. When asked by one of her friends why she married such an "ugly little man," Edith replied that he was the only man who never hurt her feelings.

William Somerset Maughm was their fifth child. Their firstborn died in infancy as did the sixth and seventh of the Maughm's children. Edith had consumption, and it was thought at the time that childbearing could cure consumption. She died within a week of her last child's death.

William Somerset Maughm, who was eight at the time of his mother's death, never recovered. Her love proved to be the only unselfish love that was ever bestowed upon him in a lifetime that spanned nearly a century. As the youngest surviving child, and with his three older brothers, Charles, Henry, and Frederic at boarding school, his mother's affection had been concentrated on him. Her death was the single most tragic experience of his life. But this was not the only tragedy of his early years. Two years after the loss of his mother, Maughm's father died of cancer, and the young Maughm was sent to live with his father's only living brother, Henry MacDonald Maughm, a church of England clergyman, in Whitstable, near Canterbury, England. With an inheritance of 150 pounds a year and a nurse to accompany him across the channel, Maughm left French soil, the country of his birth, as an orphan at the age of ten.

Speaking "fractured" French — French peppered with English phrases — Maughm arrived unhappily in Whitstable. He was ill-prepared for a strict and parsimonious household ruled by his uncle, Henry MacDonald Maughm, who was later portrayed harshly in one of his nephew's most famous novels, *Of Human Bondage*, was fond of such maxims as "Only ask those people to stay with you or dine with you who can ask you in return." Maughm spent seven years in his uncle's household, and when his taste for literature was whetted with classics such as *Alice's Adventures in Wonderland* and *The Arabian Nights*, he would have to satisfy his addiction on the sly, since his uncle disparaged him for reading so many books.

When Maughm was eleven, he was sent to the King's School in Canterbury. Here Maughm escaped the bullying of his classmates by winning prizes in music, divinity, history, and French, despite his poor showing in athletics, and, above all, the stammer that he developed shortly after arriving at his uncle's.

After acquiring the respect of his classmates with his academic achievements, he still longed for popularity and a way out of his singularly lonely existence. He would choose a boy to whom he took a particular fancy, make believe that he threw his spirit into the other boy's body, speaking with his voice and laughing with his peers in imaginary conversations. Only in this way did he find any happiness at the King's School because despite his excellence in his studies, his stammer precipitated harassment and undeserved punishment.

Maughm left the King's School in poor health and at loose ends. To the disappointment of his uncle, he decided not to go to either Cambridge or Oxford. Maughm secretly desired to become a writer, although in Victorian England being a writer was not considered a respectable way of earning a living; belief held by his uncle. His aunt, however, suggested that he spend a year in Germany with her relatives, which proved to be a turning point for Maughm.

In Germany, Maughm attended lectures at Heidelberg University, became acquainted with the works of Ibsen and Schopenhauer, and lost his virginity to a young "homosexual esthete," Ellingham Brooks, who remained a friend for the rest of his life. Maughm became convinced that he should carry out his dream of becoming a writer. Still furtively hiding his deepest convictions from his uncle, he returned to England

and at his uncle's suggestion enrolled in medical school. This gave him the opportunity to write in his spare time, unhampered, and to see life first hand—in the raw. St. Thomas's Hospital, where he spent five years, was located near Lambeth, one of London's most notorious slums.

At first, while studying for his medical degree, Maughm wrote short plays in the manner of Ibsen that portrayed the troubles of the spirit and delved into the heaviness of the heart. Obsessed with women who bear stillborn children or who die in the effort to bear children, like his mother, his first published work was a novel, entitled *Liza of Lambeth*. It was an old fashioned "potboiler," in which the heroine has an affair with a neighbor's husband, becomes pregnant, miscarries, and then dies herself when the doctor does not arrive in time. The book's only distinction was that it depicted life in a London slum to a degree that assaulted the tastes of the Victorian reading public that preferred lighter novels. Maughm was in the company of George Gissing and Arthur Morrison, who prior to Maughm, published novels regarding slum life that caused enough of a stir to inspire a few attempts to reform some of the more impoverished areas. *Liza of Lambeth* paled in comparison to the novels of Gissing and Morrison, but it launched Maughm's literary career, in 1897, at the age of twenty-three.

It would be another decade before Maughm would receive even the first glimmer of recognition. In this period, he finished six full-length plays, six novels, and a volume of short stories to ambivalent reviews and countless rejections. His travels took him to Capri, Paris, and Spain in search of material. On the continent, he hobnobbed with the famous portrait painter Gerald Kelly, the occultist Aleister Crowley, who serves as the model for the main character in his novel *The Magician*, and his old friend Ellingham Brooks. In England, he made the rounds of the cocktail circuit and kept up appearances by courting the ladies, despite the fact that his true affections lay elsewhere. The Victorian era ended and a new age was ushered in. The motto for social survival in the Edwardian era was: "Do anything you please as long as you don't scare the horses."

Maughm's long-awaited success came in 1908 with his first hit play, *Lady Frederick*. The play, a comedy about a widow who survives a financial crisis with the help of a former suitor, was one of four plays written by Maughm that ran in London's illustrious West End in the same season. A cartoon of Shakespeare biting his fingernails while a caricature of Maughm looked on appeared in the advertising spots on the broadsides of triple-decker buses. His fame, despite many caustic reviews of his work, would no longer be in doubt in his lifetime, nor after his death. And his fortune grew with his fame. Maughm grossed over four million dollars with his pen.

Shortly after his rise to literary stardom, he became involved with a young divorcee, Syrie Barnardo, whom he married in 1917, primarily because she was carrying his child. Their marriage served as a veil for his homosexuality, and eventually ended in divorce. His "real marriage" with Gerald Haxton, a fellow ambulance driver he met during service in WWI, although thinly disguised, was kept hidden for nearly three decades.

Haxton was Maughm's companion on his many excursions around the world in his fervent search for material to use in his writing. Although Haxton's alcoholism, which largely contributed to his premature death in 1944, was a nuisance, he was garrulous, outgoing, and confident—the exact opposite of Maughm, who often could not speak on the phone because of his stammer. It was Haxton, not Syrie, who accompanied him on his exploits to the South Seas, where he wrote one of his most famous short stories, "Rain," dealing with the relationship between a prostitute and a priest, and to Tahiti, where he wrote *The Moon and Sixpence*, a novel based on the life of Gauguin. During his years with Haxton, Maughm accomplished his best creative work and found a joy that was second only to his mother's love.

Through the ever-increasing sales of his books and the eventual sales of movie rights, Maughm built a home, a tribute to himself, on the French Riviera, that he called Villa Mauresque. Villa Mauresque was the site of high society parties that were frequented by Lord Beaverbrook, Sir Winston Churchill, Noel Coward, Garson Kanin, and a bevy of others who were flamboyant, glamorous, or titled.

In spite of the wealth Maughm accumulated, the avalanche of fan mail he received, and, at times, encouraging reviews of his work, he felt that he was a second-rate writer. Many of his contemporaries, such as D. H. Lawrence and Edmund Wilson, shunned him, partially because of his outrageous success. Haunted by the belief that he never realized full potential, and ailing severely from senile dementia, Maughm died ignobly at Villa Mauresque in 1965 at the age of ninety-one.

Neither severe or ignoble, Ted Morgan's biography of Maughm is an impressive work of scholarship. Of the dozen or so biographies and partial biographies extant, Morgan's is the most comprehensive and coherent. To investigate and research a life that embraces as much as Maughm's—a man who fought tenaciously to keep his life a secret—is an achievement of high praise. It is worthy of the praise that its subject deserved in life but never quite received.

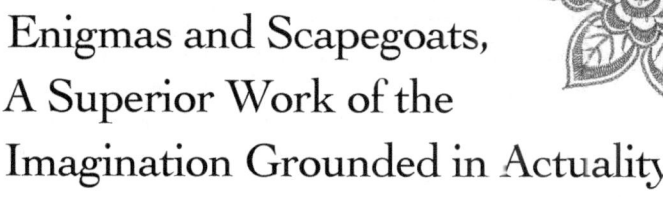

Enigmas and Scapegoats, A Superior Work of the Imagination Grounded in Actuality

Black Tickets by Jayne Anne Phillips

BLACK TICKETS IS COMPARABLE IN STATURE with such short story collections as Bernard Malamud's *The Magic Barrel*, Joyce Carol Oates's *The Poisoned Kiss*, and Tillie Olsen's *Tell Me a Riddle*. Jayne Anne Phillips writes with the poise and energy of Diane DiPrima and the force of Jack Kerouac.

The book is arranged with a story or two of only a couple of pages, or even just a paragraph, followed by a much longer piece of perhaps fifteen pages. The shorter work resembles prose poetry, although this is also a trademark of Phillips's longer stories, as well. She is consistent in crossing and recrossing the line between the standard considerations of both poetry and prose.

Phillips came of age during the 1960s and the early 1970s when the women's movement thrust itself into everyday consciousness, and she has grown with the changing roles of the new woman. Her work is androgynous. She can aptly get inside the mind of male characters, but she also portrays relationships with women, as of a mother and daughter, with a knowing compassion. She is an expert at catching fragments of social consciousness and putting them back together in stories that illuminate the state of contemporary society.

"Home," for example, is an account of a young woman who returns again to live with her mother. She is out of college, but jobless, and is presently without a lover. Her feelings are ambivalent at best about the situation, but when she arrives her mother has a job lined up for her—teaching remedial reading. She feels that at least her bank account will grow.

The daughter in the story watches her mother knit afghans and listen to Walter Cronkite and Roger Mudd on the six o'clock newscast. They argue, bicker, and cajole each other, and the daughter returns to her room at night to read current bestsellers and human interest stories in the *Reader's Digest*. Loneliness pervades the lives of both mother and daughter.

The mother is divorced, and the daughter has ghostly visions of her father sitting in the living room chair lighting cigarettes. There is no need for the mother to remarry, no need for a man. Besides, she feels, who would want her now? But her daughter quips that everyone needs "a good roll in the hay" sometimes. Tension builds throughout, primarily through their inability to communicate, although much that is discussed is communicable and understood.

Home is imbued with compassion. Neither the mother nor the daughter is a stereotype. When the daughter invites a former lover to stay at the house and the mother hears the upstairs guestroom bedsprings creaking Sunday morning on the way out the door to go to church, misunderstanding becomes explosive. When the smoke clears, mother and daughter are huddled over the kitchen sink releasing built-up tears.

Black Tickets is filled with emotion. Phillips writes with guts about gutsy situations. The world of an adolescent raised in orphanages and pulled into the somnambulant existence of two drug addicts is fixed forever in the mind of the reader of "Lechery." It is hot with eroticism and coolly indifferent, like a drug-induced stupor.

The narrator of the story, the young girl, gets herself what she needs—affection in any quantity and of any quality—to relieve the orphanage-induced loneliness. She finds lovers of all different ages, all different kinds. Wumpy, whom she met while cleaning tables at a lunch counter, pimps for her at bars, watches, but never has her himself. She woos adolescent boys with pornography and whiskey into shacks and the back seats of abandoned cars. Her voice becomes that of an adult, an older woman.

In the life she shares with Wumpy and Kitty, his lover, things are better than they were at the orphanage but still bad. While Wumpy ties up for a fix in the dark, and Kitty is nodded out, the narrator watches from the watery neon of the sign outside reflect its message across the floor—"Rooms, it says, blue Rooms." This forgotten and wasted life is sensitively exhibited by Phillips.

In one of her shorter works, "Mamasita," Phillips spins the tale of a woman who, night after night, hunts drunks with a stick outside the Men's Social Care Center. They scatter into the dark, and she swings at them as if they were rats in a broom closet. When she corners one she whacks and whacks at him while cops, walking the beat, laugh.

When she was a child, Mamasita's father locked her in a closet. Forgetting where he had put her, he opened another bottle and drank. Mamasita never forgot a motherless childhood, spent with a drunken father.

In the title story, "Black Tickets," Phillps mixes memory with desire, depicting the predicament of a jailed drug dealer who remembers and lusts after the woman who betrayed him. "Jamaica Delila," how I want you," he says in the torment of his cell, talking to himself. He turns sleepless in his cot at night wanting her body next to his, but also imagines his fist smashing into her jaw.

In his desperation, he becomes his own tormentor, playing over scenes in his mind. He remembers her body. Every detail is noted: her preference for men's clothes, the way her heels clicked on the stairs.

He met Jamaica after he was released from a Florida jail where he was doing time for statutory rape. She was selling tickets at a theater in a Philadelphia ghetto, and subsequently he and his partner, Raymond, a hunchback who dragged one foot, did their business there, making sales to "silky Main Line debs reeling in their mommy's sports cars."

He remembers nights when Jamaica could not sleep and would get up and go to the room where Raymond slept on the couch. Jealously, he watched as his partner massaged the balls of her feet. The mutiny of his lover and his friend was suspected, but he had fallen too much in love to do anything about it.

Finally, he remembers the last morning he had seen her, standing above him, cutting her hair in the shape of a bowl, and whisking the pieces over him. His last desperate hope is that she will still be around after his sentence is finished so he can even things up.

Desperation is a motif that characterizes Phillips's work. An aunt tells her niece about what it is like to do her act before the bar crowds of Denver and Cheyenne in a story, entitled "Stripper." She explains how she struts and teases the audience; loners and losers "smokin' like paper on a slow fire." "The Powder of the Angels and I'm Yours," on the other hand, deals with an ill-fated young woman and her lover who ran cocaine across the Mexican border. She sits despondently in a sanatorium watching the rain, hopelessly sewing.

Black Tickets is not an ordinary book of short fiction, and it is not written by an ordinary writer. The stories of Jayne Anne Phillips speak directly about the problems and victims of contemporary society, and Phillips gives voice to the enigmas and the scapegoats in a lacy but strong prose. *Black Tickets* is a superior work of the imagination that is grounded in actuality. No one but Phillips herself could say it better: "Characters and voices in these stories began in what is real, but became, in fact, dreams. They bear no relation to living persons, except that love or loss lends a reality to what is imagined."

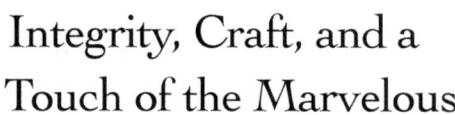

Integrity, Craft, and a Touch of the Marvelous

The Poems of Stanley Kunitz, 1923–1978

FOR MORE THAN FIFTY YEARS, THE POETRY OF Stanley Kunitz has been flowing like fresh, cool water. Unfortunately, Kunitz seems to be better known for his extracurricular activities in the world of poetry than for the poetry he has written. Kunitz has been poetry consultant to the Library of Congress and judge of the Yale Younger Poetry Prize, as well as having been the Chancellor of the Academy of American Poets.

The publication of *The Poems of Stanley Kunitz, 1928–1978* was a fortunate event in American letters. Now the bulk of the work of this careful and precise writer is available to the public in one volume. On each page there is a strong light and an ineffable vision. Kunitz's poems are a testament to living in what has been a most difficult time — the twentieth century.

"As one who was not predestined, either by nature or by art, to become a prolific poet, I must admit it pleases me that, thanks to longevity, the body of my work is beginning to acquire a bit of heft," writes Kunitz in a brief author's note prefacing the book, ostensibly stated in the humorous and humble tone that characterizes the man himself.

Kunitz has not been a prolific poet by any means, but each poem itself possess heft, each poem is a nearly perfect entity. Kunitz is an architect of music and light, and not one word is out of place in the construct of his poems. They glow from the inside out, and from outside their walls there is a celestial music. Kunitz easily stands among the peers of his generation — W. H. Auden and Theodore Roethke.

The collection leave out very few poems that Kunitz

has written. It includes poems that appeared in *Intellectual Things* (1930); *Passport to the War* (1944); *This Garland, Danger* (1958); *Selected Poems* (1958), for which he won the Pulitzer Prize; and *The Testing Tree* (1971). The poems are grouped in reverse chronological order, starting with his newest work, *The Layers: New Poems*. Kunitz has brought out collections of his work about once every ten years. For ardent readers of Stanley Kunitz it has not been often enough, but the books have always been worth the wait.

Among the twenty new poems leading off this collection, Kunitz continues with the open free verse form that marked most of *The Testing Tree*, in which he broke away from the tight iambic and the four-beat line. But Kunitz does display just how tight free verse can be. He has a fine ear for rhythm and music. In the suite of poems written on the occasion of "The Flowering of American Folk Art" exhibition at the Whitney Museum in 1974, he celebrates craftspeople such as carpenters, embroiderers, and needle pointers in such a way that his own work becomes indistinguishable from the work of the craftspeople he applauds.

The Layers: New Poems are eclectic in their topics. They range from a musing on "a cross-grained knot" that is "scored in the lintel" of his door, "bleeding through/ into the world we share" to a masterly translation from the Russian of a poem by Bella Akhmadulina, entitled "Silence." "Quinnapoxtet," a poem dusty with remembrance from Kunitz's childhood, deals with a dramatic confrontation on a Massachusetts backwoods road. The poems opens with a sensitive description of nature, portentous of what is to come:

> I was fishing in the abandoned reservoir
> back in Quinnapoxtet,
> where the snapping turtles cruised
> and the bullheads swayed
> in their bower of tree-stumps,
> slick as eels and pigeon fat.
> One of them gashed my thumb
> with a flick of his razor fin
> when I yanked the barb
> out of his gullet.
> The sun hung its terrible coals
> over Butteau's farm: I saw
> the treetops seething.

This is one of the finest passages from the new poems, exemplifying Kunitz's technical excellence and poetic vision — both of which he has incorporated into a wonderful and long-lasting marriage of half a century. Anyone unfamiliar with his work will wonder why they did not discover him sooner and will linger over each page and every poem. This is the way poetry should be read. This is the way Kunitz's poetry deservers to be read.

The title poem of the recent volume, "The Layers," is perhaps the best. It embodies the spirit of the others—remembrance of things past and change. "The Layers" is the statement of Kunitz's credo as both person and artist. He turns away from the "manic dust" of friends, "those who fell along the way," that "bitterly stings" his face. Kunitz has the will to go on in spite of the loses that have accrued on the road of life. And in such a spirit that "every stone on the road" is precious to him. The poem closes the first section of the book with such courage and confidence that all that can be believed is that there will be more road, more life lived through, and more poetry.

The Testing Tree, which was acclaimed by Robert Lowell upon its publication, is presented intact in the present collection. Every poem is worth quoting from, each is worth learning by heart.

"Journal for My Daughter," a tender love poem, is a poignant account of his relationship with his child that puts all confessional poets to shame. There is not a more moving example of compassion and understanding more beautifully written in the English language than in this nine-part poem, of which the last stanza reads:

The night when Coleridge
heavy-hearted,
bore his crying child outside,
he noted
that those brimming eyes
caught the reflection
of the starry sky,
and each suspended tear
made a sparkling moon.

What is noticed in this collection is that each poem that Kunitz writes is a love poem—whether political in content like "Around Pastor Bonhoeffer," or of a personal vein like "The Magic Curtain," a blithe account of skipping school, they are written out of love. The love is an all encompassing one. It is a love of language, a love of life.

"King of the River," an analogy between the trek of the Pacific salmon during spawning season and the process of aging in human life, is characteristic in its concerns of most of the other poems in *The Testing Tree*. Kunitz, who has witnessed the process of growing old in himself and in others, adeptly discovers that "A dry fire eats you./ Fat drips from your bones./ The flutes of your gills discolor."

Along with Kunitz's compassion, understanding, and love, there is also a sense of terror. And Kunitz writes of the terror he has known about or has seen and experienced. Poems such as "The Gladiators," which tersely depicts the brutality and inhumanity of man from the Roman games to the Children's Crusade, and "The Artist," detailing the frustrated life and eventual suicide of his friend, Mark Rothko, are striking examples.

Somehow, Kunitz has not been jaded by the darkness and bleakness surrounding him, but has been able to exercise his faculty and ability to love all the more. There are not better love poems in the modern poetry than his. The following is from "The Science of the Night," which appears in *This Garland, Danger*.

> I touch you in the night, whose gift was you,
> My careless sprawler,
> And I touch you cold, unstirring, star-bemused,
> That have become the land of your self-strangeness.
> What long seduction of the bone has led you
> Down the imploring roads I cannot take
> Into the arms of ghosts I never knew
> Leaving my manhood on a rumpled field
> To guard you where you lie so deep
> In absent-mindedness,
> Caught in the calcium snows of sleep?

"When the Light Falls," "Postscript," and "First Love" are gems in the poetic canon of the English language. They are of rare beauty. But here, also, there is much darkness of the spirit, as in "The Dark and the Fair," a poem of love gone bitter, in which Kunitz states that "We learn, as the thread plays out, that we belong/ Less to what flatters us than to what scars."

Passport to the War and *Intellectual Things* comprise poems that reflect not only Kunitz's personal life of the 1930s and the 1940s but also mirror, historically, the times. "Reflections by a Mailbox" portrays a man waiting for his "passport to the war;" "The Last Picnic," written after Pearl Harbor, concludes with the sad report that "Yesterday we had a world to lose;" and "Night Letter," a poem in which "the bloodied enveloped addressed to you./ Is history, that wide and mortal pang" are all concrete examples of Kunitz's firm social conviction and concerns. He has declared that to write a poem about war, and to succeed in doing so, is nearly impossible, because the writer is not writing something but writing about something. Clearly, Kunitz's own poems dealing with war, and its struggle, succeed in their achievement. They are potent and explosive as the reality itself. In "Careless Love," he paints an unforgettable picture of young soldiers at war, asleep, clutching their rifles.

Stanley Kunitz is a poet who writes with integrity, craft, and a touch of the marvelous. Few poets have written as well, and few poets will. The nearly 250 pages of Kunitz's poetry do not seem to be quite enough. But perfection has never been matched by quantity. *The Poems of Stanley Kunitz, 1928–1978* can be considered a classic. At the very least, Kunitz's poems are a venerable gift—like all high art they will continue to be treasured for decades to come.

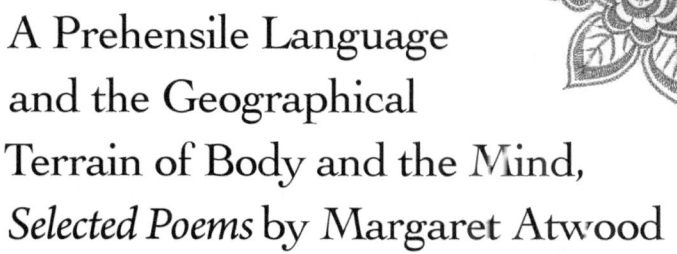

A Prehensile Language and the Geographical Terrain of Body and the Mind, *Selected Poems* by Margaret Atwood

WITHIN A PERIOD OF TIME IT WOULD TAKE TO complete one or two accomplished volumes of verse, Margaret Atwood has amassed a half dozen. In the same time she has also written a number of novels and a nonfiction guide to Canadian literature. Now her *Selected Poems* are available to be placed beside her individual volumes and for those unfamiliar with Atwood's poetry it is a fine place to start.

From the insurgent 1960s through the baffling 1970s, Atwood's razor-honed images have continued to strip any garnishes of illusion to the meanest reality. The themes have remained the same from her first book to her most recent work. A sense of history as vantage point, the constant rediscovery of the geographical terrain of the body and the mind, the quest for communication—a prehensile language, and the cosmology of relationships have all become transmitted through her work to varying degrees over the years.

Her poems spin with a dervish's energy; emotions fly up into the air, and she emblazons them onto the page.

And as tenacious as Atwood's handle on life is her grasp of language—a communicative conjuring. Sea pebbles are "as random and necessary/ as against the sky." They are a "flight of words." She says that the earliest language was not a "syntax of chained pebbles/ but liquid made/ by the first tribes, the fish/ people."

Despite this strong conviction and commitment to words as things, there are times when she considers them obsolete, at least metaphorically, as in one of her spiritual odysseys, "Journey to the Interior:"

A compass is useless, also
trying to take directions
from the movements of the sun,
which are erratic;
and words here are as pointless
as calling in a vacant
wilderness.

The poet sees the universe as it is—in constant motion, eddying around our daily lives. In her struggle to find something stable, to locate that elusive center of things, of oneself, she discovers:

There is no center;
the centers
travel with us unseen
like our shadows
on a day when there is no sun.

This is itself a center. This understanding is at the matrix of being. Circles are broken, animals, men, and matter are transformed and become something else. This is an underlying belief in her struggle for survival. And Atwood knows that "in order to survive/ we make what we can and have to/ with what we have."

The realization that there is little that is black and white, that much of what we see falls into a gray area does not hinder Atwood's articulation. Paradoxically, she focuses her vision through life's perennial ebb and flow as if she were a comic book superhero with x-ray vision. The "too-fixed stare" of "wide windows," for example, "give momentary access to/ the landscape behind or under/ the future cracks in the plaster."

It is hardly enough to walk around something either at hand or at a distance. In "Against Still Life," for instance, an orange is "in the middle of a table." As usual, Atwood wants it to say more than just "orange" to her. She "wants to be told/ everything it has to say." Through her craving for the unraveling of the center of things, the syrup of existence, she conjures the silence of the orange to that of her lover, sitting in the same room. But here again, the writer charts the uncharted like a sensual mystery. If the orange is taken gently in the palm of your hand, you may find:

an egg
a sun
an orange moon

perhaps a skull; center
of all energy

By the same token, if she observes her lover patiently, long enough, there's a chance he might say, even silently, to her that:

there are mountains
inside your skull
garden and chaos, ocean
and hurricane; certain
corners of rooms, portraits
of great-grandmothers, curtains
of a particular shade;
your deserts; your private
dinosaurs; the first
woman?

Hence, the provocative quality of invocation in her poetry is carried to even greater heights in *The Journals of Susanna Moodie*, which also is included in *Selected Poems*. Moodie, an early pioneer and settler in the Canadian wilderness, is invoked in such a way that much more than her guise and her persona are taken on. Atwood's shamanistic capabilities come into fruition here in almost an eerie manner.

"I am a word/ in a foreign language" states Moodie in "Journal I." The wilderness that she entered with her husband, she refers to as her "own ignorance." Scraping a living out of the wilderness becomes a miasma of hallucination for Susanna Moodie. Caught up in the trials of the frontier she remarks that "whether the wilderness is/ real or not/ depends on who lives there."

Here is Atwood's investment in history's vantage point on display — her own scraping for roots as Susanna Moodie scrounged the woods for the tubers of edible plants. Atwood herself has had her taste of the Canadian back country; she was born there in 1939. But through *The Journals of Susanna Moodie*, Atwood investigates her national origin as if she were witnessing the immigrants' struggle herself, for the first time, through the eyes of her heroine.

A tragic motif continues throughout the range of action in the bush country. In "Death of Young Son by Drowning," Moodie finally must accept the haunting landscape that surrounds her as she retrieves her son's body. She says of him that he was the "cairn of my plans and future charts," as he was pulled from the river "with poles and hooks/ from among the nudging logs." Now Moodie seems to have become inured by this last proverbial straw, and she says with head raised high that she "planted him in this country/ like a flag."

As with Christ's forty days spent in the desert, here too, transcendence has occurred. Moodie speaks coldly, soberly, with mystic comprehension of her milieu. A bear moving toward her family's cabin becomes "a mute vibration passing/ between her ears." She has accrued an otherworldly sense, and intuition, a primal magic and knowledge. She grieves, though, for her "disintegrated children," with her whole body; her arms, her eyes. When she walks along the overgrown path her "skirt/ is tugged at by the spreading briers." And her lost children "catch at her heels with their fingers."

On her deathbed, Moodie becomes solipsistic, but not so much in a pejorative sense, as in a strong Whitmanesque conviction. "What will they do now/ that I, that all/ depending on me disappears?" she asks. Susanna Moodie struggled with the land, and through that confrontation over the years transcendence took place within her. The land has become Susanna Moodie, Susanna Moodie has become the land — a oneness has been achieved.

With the selections from the volumes *Procedures for Underground*, *Power Politics*, and *You Are Happy*, Atwood returns to her own persona. In these poems, she turns her concern to relationships and their inherent problems. Almost ruefully, she states that "Marriage is not/ a house or even a tent." It is something that possibly happened at the end of the ice age beside the retreat of a glacier "where painfully and with wonder/ at having survived even/ this far/ we are learning to make fire."

Again, we have Atwood's instinct for survival metaphorically positioned on a rugged geographical terrain that has spoken to and for a generation that has evolved in those emotional regions over the past however many cataclysmic years. She confronts the ferocity of love with as much ferocity. Much of what is experienced is sham, artifice, trickery. And her poems are chiseled, finely etched.

the ceiling opens
a voice sings Love Is A Many

Splendoured Things
you hang suspended above the city

in blue tights and a red cape,
your eyes flashing in unison.
As for me, I continue eating;

I liked you better the way you were,
but you were always ambitious.

Lack of understanding and truth, and the denial of feelings — love's aggressors, the nemesis of relationships are portrayed here. When understanding a partner is "anything/ but that and to avoid it." And of truth, she says "should exists/ it should not be used/ like this. If I love you/ is that a fact or a weapon?"

Atwood's voice echoes with universal admonition: "Next time we commit/ love, we ought to/ choose in advance what/ to kill." This is not so much bitterness as it is an adult lesson learned the hard way, as if after having to write it on the blackboard of the heart after hours.

Through her last book, though, an apotheosis of celebration is reached through an intense lyricism. "Circe/ Mud Poems," a sequence of poems incorporated in *You Are Happy*, implements the Greek myth of Circe and Odysseus. This time the terrain on which the poems take place is a desert island. Possibly it is a replica of Aeaea, where before Circe fell in love with Odysseus, she fed acorns to his men, and through her powers changed them into swine. But here is another emotional battleground, where more transformations occur, and the renewed conviction in love is upheld like a flag:

My face, my other faces
stretching over it like
rubber, like flowers opening
and closing, like rubber,
like liquid steel,
like steel. Face of steel.

Margaret Atwood is a convincing and prolific poet — convincing in her language, prolific in the accuracy of its use. Her *Selected Poems* is an appropriate tribute to her talent as a poet of major accomplishments — on the world stage.

About the Author

Wally Swist is the author of over forty books and chapbooks of poetry and prose.

Among his books, he has published *The Daodejing: A New Interpretation*, along with coauthors, David Breeden and Steven Schroeder (Beaumont, TX: Lamar University Press, 2015). Also, his book *Huang Po and the Dimensions of Love*, was selected as the co-winner of the 2011 Crab Orchard Series Open Poetry Contest, which was chosen by Pulitzer Prize-winning poet Yusef Komunyakaa, who served as judge, and the book was published by Southern Illinois University Press, in 2012. The book was nominated for a National Book Award.

Swist is the winner of the 2018 Ex Ophidia Press Poetry Prize for *A Bird Who Seems to Know Me: Poems and Haiku Regarding Birds and Nature*. The book was published in late 2019 by master printer and book designer Gabriel Rummonds, of Bainbridge Island, Washington.

He has also published six books of poetry from Shanti Arts, LLC, of Brunswick, Maine, including *Candling the Eggs* (2016), *The Map of Eternity* (2018), *The Bees of the Invisible* (2019), *Evanescence: Selected Poems* (2020), *Awakening and Visitation* (2020), and *Taking Residence* (2021).

His books of nonfiction include *Singing for Nothing: Selected Nonfiction as Literary Memoir* (Brooklyn, NY: The Operating System, 2018) and *On Beauty: Essays, Reviews, Fiction, and Plays* (New York and Lisbon: Adelaide Books, 2018). The latter book's eponymous essay "On Beauty" was the recipient of first prize in the Adelaide Books Literary Awards for the essay category, which was collected in *Adelaide Literary Awards Anthology: Essays 2018* (New York and Lisbon: Adelaide Books, 2019).

Some of Swist's work has been set to music, including the poems "Geese Landing" and "Swallows" that were set to music for piano and soprano by Dr. Douglas Bruce Johnson. A performance of the music and the poems was held at Trinity College, Hartford, Connecticut, where, for nearly a quarter century, Dr. Johnson was Associate Professor of Music.

Other poetry that has been set to music includes "The Rush of the Brook Stills the Mind," which inspired a composition by the electroacoustic composer Dr. Elainie Lillios. The composition was performed by percussionist Scott Deal in Jordan Hall at the New England Conservatory of Music in Boston, Massachusetts, on June 20, 2013. It is only one of several venues across the country where the composition has been performed. Dr. Elainie Lillios is Professor of Composition at Bowling Green State University.

"After Long Drought" was also composed to an electroacoustical score written by Professor Elainie Lillios, and the composition was also premiered at Jordan Hall at the New England Conservatory of Music in June 2016 by percussionist Scott Deal.

Swist is a recipient of Artist's Fellowships in poetry from the Connecticut Commission on the Arts (1977 and 2003). He was also awarded a one-year writing residency (1998) and two back-to-back one-year writing residencies (2003–2005) at Fort Juniper, the Robert Francis Homestead, in Cushman, Massachusetts.

His work has appeared in national periodicals such as *Commonweal, The North American Review, Rattle, Rolling Stone, Your Impossible Voice*, and *Yankee Magazine*.

Swist makes his home in New England, where he is semi-retired and works as a freelance editor, writer, and researcher.

www.ingramcontent.com/pod-product-compliance
Lightning Source LLC
Chambersburg PA
CBHW061524020726
47502CB00006B/2225